Guidelines for extrasensory perception research

Julie Milton
and Richard Wiseman

Supported by
The John Björkhem
Memorial Foundation

University of Hertfordshire Press

First published 1997 in
Great Britain by
University of Hertfordshire Press
Learning Resources Centre
University of Hertfordshire
College Lane, Hatfield
Hertfordshire AL10 9AB

ISBN 0-900458-74-7

Cover design by
Lisa Cordes

Cover illustration
© Ingram Pinn

Page layout by
Emma Greening

Printed by
Watkiss Studios Limited

Contents

Acknowledgements

This research was funded by the John Björkhem Memorial Foundation. We are grateful to Paul Kurtz, Tony Lawrence, Bob Morris, John Palmer, Paul Stevens and Caroline Watt for useful information and commentary, and to those colleagues who took part in a questionnaire survey concerning the importance of certain methodological safeguards discussed in this book. We are also grateful to Bill Forster, Emma Greening and Lisa Cordes for helping with the production of the book.

Foreword

It is generally agreed by proponent and sceptic alike that parapsychology in recent years has made considerable methodological progress, both in detecting and eliminating fraud and in the use of more sophisticated research procedures to eliminate unintended artefact. Richard Wiseman and I attempted to address the first set of issues, especially as they apply to those who might always attempt fraud, in an earlier book, *Guidelines for Testing Psychic Claimants*. The present work, by Julie Milton and Richard Wiseman, attempts to cover both sets of issues, specifically for experimental research in the area of extrasensory perception, or ESP.

The authors present a remarkably thorough cataloguing of the steps needed in designing and conducting a good ESP experiment, plus a good discussion of their justification. Not all issues of method are resolved in parapsychology and the authors do not pretend otherwise. They do not cover certain specialised areas such as psychophysiological measurement or research with animals as there are many issues that are particular to those areas and that call for familiarity with the methodological literature from these areas themselves. Nor do they cover issues arising in complex experimental designs, as once again there exists a detailed literature on experimental design that generalises nicely to parapsychological procedures.

The authors have tried to focus on what is unique to ESP experimental research and on what is necessary to avoid the kinds of criticism that are generally directed at such research. They have brought together in one place the information available only from many separate publications and have organised it in a very practical way so that it would be easy to apply. Thus this treatise can be useful for the methodology student, the general parapsychology student and even the student of areas related to parapsychology. It is also an invaluable aid for the practical researcher in planning and conducting research, as well as the evaluator who must read a proposal or completed research report and form an opinion of its worth. It is also therefore a handy item to have around when reading the work of colleagues or doing literature reviews, including meta-analyses that incorporate coding for flaws. As noted at the start, parapsychology has made progress in its methods and the availability of this document is an important step in ensuring that those advances can be available to all, from the senior researcher to the novice, including researchers from other disciplines who decide to try doing studies in this area. Often we carry with us an assumption that if we know how to do research in our own areas we will, of course, have no problem in figuring out how to do it in cognate fields. But Milton and Wiseman show us here that there are many traps in ESP research that are not so obvious as we might think. They have done a service to all.

Professor Robert L. Morris
Koestler Chair of Parapsychology
University of Edinburgh
August, 1996.

Introduction

Many researchers are interested in assessing the quality of published extrasensory perception experiments or wish to carry out studies of their own. It is clearly important that such individuals are aware of the methodological pitfalls that can occur during this type of work and some of the ways in which these problems can be overcome. Unfortunately, the literature discussing these issues is extensive and scattered throughout many different books and journals.

This manual addresses this problem by presenting methodological guidelines for the common types of ESP experiment. We do not, however, cover the highly specialised safeguards required for the more unusual types of experimental design, such as studies in which the participant's physiological state is monitored for changes in response to some hidden stimulus, or studies in which participants attempt to describe the contents of a hidden picture in terms of a coding system (the presence or absence of people, or of buildings and so on). Such studies have a methodological literature of their own which is too large to cover here.

It should be noted that the guidelines do not just apply to purely "proof-oriented" studies - now rare - in which the sole aim of the study is to demonstrate the existence of ESP by close attention to ruling out methodological artefact. The safeguards are for the most part equally relevant in most "process-oriented" research, that is, research whose purpose is to examine relationships between ESP performance and some other variable or variables. Researchers sometimes assume that if a process-oriented study has methodological weaknesses then all participants will exploit them, consciously or not, to an equal degree. Thus, any statistically significant difference between the ESP scores of two groups in such a study is taken to indicate a genuine relationship between the variable in question and ESP performance. However, in many cases the relationships obtained between ESP scores and psychological variables are the same as would be expected if participants were instead responding to some weak sensory stimulus (Palmer, 1978), so if the participant is not adequately screened from the target, the lack of safeguards becomes a plausible explanation for the results. This issue is discussed in more detail in Milton (1995a). Suffice it to say here that we recommend that those involved in process-oriented research take the guidelines as seriously as they would if conducting proof-oriented research.

These guidelines are not intended to be a set of rules that people are forced to follow but rather a thorough, useful and convenient information resource to help experimenters and evaluators make informed choices in the design, reporting and assessment of ESP experiments. Neither are the guidelines intended as a primer. Researchers unfamiliar with experimental design in parapsychology are recommended first to read some introductory material on this subject (e.g. Morris, 1978; Palmer, 1986a) and to examine the designs of recently published ESP studies in the main specialist journals.

Chapter 1 Basic experimental designs in ESP research

In all ESP experiments, a *target* is selected from a set of alternatives by a random method for each trial. A *receiver* (usually referred to in parapsychological literature just as a 'participant' or 'subject') attempts to guess the identity of the target and his or her response is recorded. The response and target are then compared and the outcome of the trial (i.e. whether the response was correct) is noted. After all the experiment's trials have been completed, the number of correct guesses obtained is compared statistically with the number expected by chance (in most studies, the relationship between ESP performance and other variables is also examined statistically and may be the main focus of the study).

Clairvoyance, telepathy and precognition

There are three basic types of ESP study. A *clairvoyance* study requires the receiver in each trial to guess the identity of a hidden target that is not known to anyone else. A *telepathy* study (usually called a 'general ESP' or GESP study by parapsychologists) requires the receiver to guess the identity of a target whose content is known to another person, the *sender* (often referred to in the literature as the 'agent'). A *precognition* experiment requires the receiver to guess the identity of a target that will be randomly chosen only after the receiver has made his or her response.

Forced-choice and free-response studies

There are two common formats for all of these types of study. In a *forced-choice* study, the receiver knows the target alternatives (e.g. 'cross' or 'circle', or '0' or '1') before he or she makes a guess. At the end of the experiment the number of correct guesses made by receivers can be compared with chance expectation using the binomial distribution, or an approximation to it. In a *free-response* study the receiver only knows what type of item the target might be (e.g. any picture, any object, any geographical location). The receiver is asked to describe the target by describing the thoughts and images (*mentation*) that occur to him or her during the response period and a record is made of this mentation. Clearly, almost any mentation record would have at least some similarity to almost any target and so it is necessary to use control targets to allow the use of statistical methods similar to those employed in forced-choice studies. Each trial's mentation record is therefore compared with each item in a *target set* composed of the target and several decoys, the comparison being made by a *judge* who is blind to the target's identity. The receiver might perform this task before being informed of the target's identity or it might be carried out by an *independent judge* who has no other connection with the study. The judge must attempt to identify the target by choosing the single item in each target set that best corresponds to the mentation record (or must rank or rate the items in order of correspondence, in many studies). Appropriate statistical tests are then used to determine whether the experiment's outcome exceeds chance expectation.

It is usual in forced-choice experiments for each receiver to do many trials, each taking a few seconds, often in a single session. In free-response experiments, an entire experimental session of half an hour or more is usually devoted to a single trial and receivers often contribute only one or a few trials to an experiment. A forced-choice study typically consists of hundreds or thousands of trials, whereas free-response studies frequently involve fewer than a hundred.

Open-deck and closed-deck studies

There are two ways of selecting target series for ESP studies - *open-deck* and *closed-deck*. Each manifests itself differently in forced-choice and free-response studies with each method requiring different safeguards.

In forced-choice open-deck studies, the probability of each trial's target being chosen is independent of what targets have been chosen on the other trials, as though targets were being selected from a very large mix of target choices, with replacement. In closed-deck forced-choice studies, however, there is a fixed number of each target alternative and they are sampled without replacement. For example, a run of twenty-five trials might consist of exactly five of each of five target types, and the probability of any target type being selected for a given trial would depend on how many of each had already been chosen.

In free-response open-deck studies, a large pool of different target items (e.g. 100 different pictures) is divided into fixed target sets (e.g. twenty-five sets of four pictures). The target set is randomly selected for each trial and a target is randomly selected from within the target set. In a *closed-deck* study, the large target pool is not divided into fixed sets and each trial does not have an individual target set. Instead, each trial's target is selected randomly from the whole pool, without replacement, and at the end of the experiment the targets that were selected for each trial are combined to form a target set. So, for example, if there were ten trials in the study there will be ten items in the target set (closed-deck free-response studies usually involve very small numbers of trials). The judge must then attempt to match each trial's mentation record with the appropriate target.

Stages in ESP studies

We can use a forced-choice clairvoyance study as an example to illustrate the sequence of events in a typical ESP experiment. First, a set of barriers is erected to prevent normal channels of communication between target and receiver. The exact form of these barriers changes as the study progresses but to begin with they consist of the precautions that the experimenters take to prevent the receiver, or anyone who might communicate with him or her, from observing the target selection process. Next, a seqence of targets is randomly selected for either just the next session or for the whole study. The target sequence might be in the form of a list on a sheet of paper (of digits, symbols, words and so on) or a sequence of stimuli on a computer screen or, more rarely these days, a deck of cards bearing special symbols. Communication barriers are kept in place by keeping the selected targets secure from the receiver until and during the experimental session. Frequently in clairvoyance studies the target sequence is displayed or set apart from other material in some way during the session, but with barriers in place so that no one can see it. For example, a list of the sequence might be set alone on a table, in a sealed, opaque envelope or a computer might display the sequence on its screen in a locked, guarded and visually shielded room. At this time, the receiver attempts to guess the target sequence and his or her responses are recorded. The responses are compared with the targets and the experimenter notes whether each trial's response is correct (a 'hit') or not (a 'miss'). Finally, the experiment's results are compared with chance expectation using the appropriate statistic.

Chapter 2 Pre-specification of experimental details and statistical tests

Even before a study begins, certain safeguards are necessary to ensure that experimenters will not be free to ignore data that does not conform to their hypotheses. This potential problem of post-hoc data selection and analysis in ESP research has been recognised since the earliest days of the Rhine era. Clearly, if experimenters are free to choose which trials to include in an analysis or which of several possible measures of ESP performance to use once they know the experimental results, then the experiment's outcome could be considerably inflated. The selection need not be deliberate; failure to remember clearly which trials were to be included or which analyses were intended could alone lead to problems. The following sections recommend procedures to avoid such pitfalls.

Pre-specification of sample size

'Optional stopping' describes a situation in which an experimenter chooses when to stop collecting data rather than having pre-specified the number of trials in a study. If an experimenter could choose to terminate an experiment after a series of successful trials it would be possible to make a null effect statistically significant. Optional stopping in some early ESP studies attracted attention from commentators such as Leuba (1938) and Greenwood (1938) who demonstrated empirically how powerful such a strategy could be in boosting a study's apparent level of success.

Akers (1984) and Lemmon (1939) recommended pre-specification of sample size in order to rule out optional stopping and pre-specification of sample size was a meta-analytic quality criterion for Honorton and Ferrari (1989), Lawrence (1993) and Milton (1993)[1]. Alternatively, the decision to stop collecting data could be made by someone blind to the receiver's performance (Milton, 1993).

Occasionally, experimenters run extra trials in a study, for example as back-up trials in case once the study is over there turn out to be problems with some of its trials. In this situation, we recommend pre-specification of whether to include these extra trials if they are not needed.

Pre-specification of pilot and formal trials

Some studies, including the early experiments of J.B. Rhine, have been criticised because their authors did not make it clear that they had determined in advance which trials were to be classed as experimental trials and which were to be classed as practice, pilot or exploratory trials.

Hyman (1985) noted a similar problem in his critique of the ganzfeld database (a collection of ESP studies using a special sensory habituation environment for their participants). He was concerned that if experimenters do not pre-specify the status of trials clearly, then some experimenters might decide to treat pilot or exploratory series of trials as constituting a formal study to be published if the trials were successful but would not report them otherwise. This form of post-hoc data selection would tend to inflate the overall success rate of formal studies as a group.

Hyman called for studies to be clearly labelled as either exploratory (designed to generate testable hypotheses) or confirmatory (designed to confirm or reject the hypotheses generated by the exploratory studies), a recommendation supported by Honorton (Hyman and Honorton, 1986). Hyman further recommended the publication of exploratory studies only when they were providing context for the results of a confirmatory study.

---

[1]Meta-analysts of parapsychological databases have frequently coded studies in terms of their methodological quality in order to attempt to detect any association between effect size and methodological weakness. Although they have generally not discussed their choice of quality criteria and have rarely made explicit recommendations for future experimental practice, their quality criteria nevertheless represent implicit minimum procedural recommendations and will be treated as such in this book.

Pre-specification of statistical tests

In addition, experimenters are widely recommended to pre-specify exactly which statistical test, including the level of alpha, will be applied to exactly which data to test any particular hypothesis (Akers, 1984; Honorton and Ferrari, 1989; Hyman and Honorton, 1986; Lawrence, 1993; Milton, 1993, 1994; Palmer, 1986b). In forced-choice studies the use of the binomial distribution for the study's overall outcome is so common that experimenters may consider it unnecessary to state that the analysis was pre-planned. However, other methods are possible such as using the participant, rather than the trial as the unit of analysis. Pre-specification of analysis is therefore recommended even for forced-choice studies.

Akers (1984) and Hansel (1980) also recommend that if analyses involve examining the relationship between ESP performance and a participant's classification in terms of some other variable, the classification criteria should be specified in writing in advance of the experiment. For example, if the experimenter is using a five-point scale in order to classify participants into two groups, then he or she should pre-specify the cut-off criteria in terms of the scale.

In some studies, experimenters report several outcome measures to test a single hypothesis. For example, in free-response studies the overall outcome can be assessed in terms of 'direct hits' (the number of times the target was correctly selected), 'binary hits' (the number of times the target was ranked in the top half of the judging set) and a number of other measures. With these multiple measures there is a risk that experimenters might report only the successful ones, thus inflating the study's outcome, or might interpret a study as successful when correction for multiple analysis would have shown that it was not (Hyman, 1985; Honorton, 1985).

Hyman and Honorton (1986) jointly recommended that appropriate adjustments should be made when multiple tests are planned and it makes sense that the choice of method should be pre-specified. However, the Bonferroni method of correction that they use as an example (Rosenthal and Rubin, 1984) is very conservative. Experimenters may therefore prefer Kennedy's (1979a) recommendation that experimenters pre-specify a single statistical analysis for the study's outcome, a solution that both avoids the need for correction and accidental selective reporting.

Pre-specification of randomness tests
Concerns about post-hoc data selection and multiple analysis apply equally to the choice of data and statistical tests used to determine whether the target sequence is random or is from a random parent population. If experimenters are free to choose data and tests post-hoc, they might find themselves open to accusations of avoiding applying tests that would have shown up some non-randomness in the ouput, or might give the impression that a post-hoc test that obtains a statistically significant result is more important that it actually is. There appear to be no published recommendations that randomness tests should be pre-specified but such pre-specification is a common requirement in tests more directly related to the experimental hypotheses and we recommend it.

Registration of pre-specified procedures
Although commentators recommend pre-specification to rule out data selection, it is not clear what safeguards they would require to be sure that such pre-specification had actually taken place. Some commentators stipulate that they would require the specifications to have been made in writing. Some consumers of parapsychological research might also prefer that experimenters register the written pre-specifications of procedures for their studies with someone who is uninvolved with the experiment, before data collection begins. Although we are aware that some researchers register details of planned analyses and other key procedures with others, this is not something that often appears in experimental reports and we are not aware of any published discussion on this matter. However, since written pre-specification would be helpful to the experimenter and, once written, it is easy to register the pre-specifications with someone else, we recommend both these safeguards.

Chapter 3 Methods of randomisation

Because most ESP experiments measure their success by comparing the number of hits obtained with the theoretical mean chance expectation, adequate randomisation is crucial. It is well known that participants in forced-choice ESP experiments do not produce random strings of guesses: indeed, most people asked to produce random sequences cannot do so (e.g. Budescu, 1987) without special training (Schouten, 1975). If the target sequence, as well as the call sequence, was non-random, the statistical assumptions underlying the use of probability theory in this context would be violated. Clearly, some method other than simple human choice must be used to generate target sequences, not only because a non-random sequence would be likely but also because the randomiser's sequence might be related to the receiver's call sequence because of similarities in their psychologies or in their environment.

This is more probable than one might think. People tend to be highly stereotypical in their selection of a number or picture (e.g. Marks and Kammann, 1980) so that it is not unlikely that two people will make similar choices in the same order. This becomes even more likely if there is something in their shared environment that might predispose them both to a particular target option. It is especially important that senders in telepathy studies should not be allowed to choose targets because in addition to this problem of unintentional non-independence of targets and responses, there would also be the possibility that the sender and receiver might have planned to cheat by pre-arranging a target sequence for both to produce (Akers, 1984; Hansen, 1990). Researchers have used a variety of methods to generate target sequences and the following sections discuss their strengths and weaknesses.

Dice-throwing, card-shuffling and drawing lots
In the early ESP research of the 1930s, the shuffling of cards and the throwing of dice were the most common means of target randomisation. Dice-throwing is known to produce non-random sequences of numbers unless specially constructed dice are used. With most dice, the '6' face is more likely to fall upwards than the others, followed by the 5, 4, 3, 2, and 1 faces, because the faces are made by scooping small pits out of the surface so that the higher-numbered faces have less mass than the rest. The control data from dice-throwing PK experiments show this effect clearly (Radin and Ferrari, 1991). Using cards also has disadvantages. Although they can be shuffled in such a way as to produce adequately random sequences (Epstein, 1967), success depends upon such factors as the number of shuffles, the skill of the shuffler, the consistency of the shuffler's performance, the amount of wear on the cards and so on.

For these reasons, most commentators do not favour using these or other informal methods of randomisation such as drawing lots (e.g. Akers, 1984; Honorton and Ferrari, 1989; Honorton, 1985; Hyman, 1985; Lawrence, 1993; Milton, 1993, 1994; see also Fienberg, 1971 and Rosenblatt and Filliben, 1971 for an interesting account of how the failure of drawing lots to produce a random selection of birthdates for the Vietnam war draft led to a series of lawsuits).

Mechanical and electronic random number generators
Mechanical 'random number generators' (RNGs), mostly machines designed to shuffle cards or throw dice in a random way (e.g. Tyrrell, 1938), were designed to improve upon these informal methods of randomisation. Mechanical RNGs have all but vanished from ESP research but before their disappearance they were joined by electronic RNGs, still-popular devices that operate by sampling the output of a radioactive source or of a noise diode (e.g. Schmidt, 1970). These electronic RNGs are sometimes referred to as 'true' RNGs to distinguish them from pseudo-RNGs (described later).

Although an improvement on earlier methods, both mechanical and electronic REGs have their own potential problems. Some problems are specific to the type of RNG: the cards in card-shuffling machines can become worn so that randomness tests on their earlier output may not represent the later output, and dice-throwing machines can only be as unbiased as the dice used with them. Both mechanical and electronic devices can develop intermittent faults, have design flaws and be susceptible to environmental influences. Depending upon the type of RNG, these influences can include vibration, air currents, humidity changes, temperature changes, transient magnetic field changes, power spikes and warm-up effects (e.g. Davis and Akers, 1974; May, Humphrey and Hubbard, 1980). Nelson, Dunne and Jahn (1988) even considered the possibility that their very large 'Random Mechanical Cascade', an RNG roughly 2m wide and 3m high through which plastic balls bounce on their way down through a matrix of pins into collecting bins, might be susceptible to the effects of gravitation and the tides.

When reporting details of a mechanical or electronic RNG it is therefore important to give enough details of the RNG so that the reader can assess the likelihood of design problems and susceptibility to environmental influences. For mechanical RNGs this would include construction details such as diagrams, plans and so on. For electronic RNGs this information would include details of the physics, circuitry and constructed parameters of the RNG (May, Humphrey and Hubbard, 1980) or, if it is a commerical one, the model name and that of any computer interfaced with it, with a reference to its fuller documentation (Hyman and Honorton, 1986).

Pseudo-RNGs

Pseudo-random number generators (pseudo-RNGs) are algorithms that aim to produce a series of numbers with the characteristics of a 'truly' random sequence while being produced by a deterministic method.

Pseudo-RNGs are, of course, not susceptible to environmental influences, mechanical breakdowns and so on. However, not all commonly available pseudo-RNGs produce adequately random output. Several authors (Hansen, 1987; Hyman and Honorton, 1986; Radin, 1985) have warned against the use of microcomputer random functions because their algorithms are rarely documented and many are unsatisfactory (Modianos, Scott and Cornwell, 1984). Radin also points out that, although there are algorithms whose output is acceptably random in theory, computers have limited precision in their calculations and may therefore produce unacceptable output from such algorithms in practice. Also, computers differ in their precision so that the same algorithm may produce different output on different machines.

For these reasons, it is important to report sufficient detail about an pseudo-RNG for the reader to be confident of two things: that the algorithm produces acceptably random output and that the output produced by it in the experiment is drawn from the same parent output as has been tested for randomness. If the experimenter ran his or her own tests on the pseudo-RNG under the same hardware and software conditions as obtained in the experiment, then it is sufficient to report the pseudo-RNG programme and details of the statistical tests conducte upon it (or give references to this information). Otherwise, the experimenter will have to demonstrate that the programme is producin the same output under the experimental conditions as it did in the randomness tests. It is possible to do this by reporting certain technical information (the programming language and version number; the computer model and microprocessor type; the random access memory available; the operating system and version number; the degree of arithmetic precision used in the algorithm programme and so on), but this information can be difficult to find. Radin (1985) points out that researchers can more simply show whether their algorithm is producin the same output as it did when tested for randomness by comparing the first fifty numbers generated by it for a particular seed number under both randomness testing and experimental conditions.

Hyman and Honorton (1986) recommend reporting the method of obtaining the seed number. When the randomiser uses a single seed number to produce a sequence of targets for the whole experiment, it i relatively unimportant that the means of producing the seed number m be slightly non-random, so using dice throws or coin flips for this purpose is acceptable. However, in some open-deck free-response studies, the randomiser produces a seed number for each trial's target. In this situation, the use of informal means of randomisation in order t select the seed number could result in bias in target frequency at least. Consider the extreme case of a dice so loaded that it always rolls a six. This would result in the target in the same position in the target set being chosen for every trial in the experiment. The randomness tests carried out on the pseudo-RNG would clearly be irrelevant. We therefore recommend that randomisers either use an adequately rando means of producing a seed number (such as using a tested electronic RNG), or that they avoid this trial-by-trial selection of targets.

Random number tables

Random number tables, not being subject to mechanical breakdown, environmental conditions or computing limitations, are a popular and convenient choice for ESP experiments. Some tables used by researchers in the past have attracted criticism for not being adequately random (Spencer-Brown, 1957). The RAND Corporation tables (RAND Corporation, 1955), the most frequently used in parapsychology, appear to be free from such problems (but see the section on output coding in the next chapter). Davis and Akers (1974) point out that when using random number tables, digits should be used in the order in which the tables were tested for randomness (usually along rows rather than down columns) because 'tables are only as good as the tests made upon them' (p.397).

Because random number tables have been so variable in quality, Hyman and Honorton (1986) recommend reporting the reference of the table used along with the exact method of determining the entry point. If a different entry point is chosen for each trial, rather than a single entry point determining the target sequence for the whole study, then we recommend, as we did for pseudo-RNG seed numbers in such a case, that randomisers avoid using an informal means of choosing the entry point such as dice-throwing or coin-tossing. Alternatively, a single entry point could be used for the whole study using an informal method.

Randomiser details

Whatever source of randomness is used, someone must perform the randomisation unless the process is fully automated. Hyman and Honorton (1986) recommend reporting details of the training, supervision and qualifications of student experimenters in ganzfeld studies. This suggests that the relevant training and qualifications of anyone who carries out an experimental procedure in any type of ESP study should be reported, including those of the personnel who carry out the randomisation procedure.

Chapter 4 Randomness testing

The problems outlined in the previous chapter could result in a non-random selection of ESP targets. For this reason it is important that researchers carry out randomisation tests and that the results of these tests are properly documented and reported.

When, how and where tests should be conducted

Davis and Akers (1974) recommend extensive tests on electronic RNGs before they are placed into service with regular tests thereafter. They also suggest that control tests on electronic RNGs be run before and after the experiment and/or at a convenient break during the experiment. Some experimenters run more frequent checks, perhaps alternating control runs with experimental runs or in counterbalanced order with the experimental runs, as suggested by Hansel (1981) and Hyman (1981).

Several authors have suggested that tests on RNGs be conducted in the expermental test environment and under similar conditions to those used in the actual experiment. In this way, any factors that might affect the RNG's output (such as the switching on or off of fluorescent lights near the RNG, the passage of trains outside the building, the presence of peripheral devices attached to the RNG and so on) remain constant during the experimental and control runs (Akers, 1984, Davis and Akers, 1974). For the same reason, Davis and Akers recommend that RNGs should not be run at rates in experiments in excess of those at which they were tested. During any multiple-block randomisation tests (i.e. tests in which multiple blocks of output roughly the same length as the experimental series are tested for randomness), some experimenters prefer to have the RNG switched on and running for each block only for the same period of time as it is during the experimental trials in order to detect any transient effects on the device when it is switched on and off and warming up.

Davis and Akers also recommend that randomisation tests be repeated if the RNG is modified or replaced.

Choice of output: Global or local?

There are two types of RNG output that are commonly tested for randomicity in ESP studies. A series of output much longer than the experimental target sequence can be subjected to 'global' randomness tests, or the experimental series itself (or a number of blocks of output the same length as the experimental series) can be subjected to 'local' tests. Hyman (Hyman and Honorton, 1986) favours a third alternative known as the 'empirical cross-check' which was used in early card-guessing experiments (Rhine et al., 1966). In this method, each target in the experimental series itself is compared with a receiver's response intended for another trial. If randomisation is adequate, these control comparisons should yield means and standard deviations consistent with the theoretical distribution based on the null hypothesis.

Tart and Dronek (1982) provide an argument against relying on tests performed only on the experimental target sequence itself in trial-by-trial feedback studies. They demonstrate that if an RNG is biased and standard chi-square tests of randomness are restricted to the experimental target sequence or a control sequence of the same length, the magnitude of the obtained chi-square is a very poor measure of the results that a receiver could obtain by using a mathematical inference strategy if he or she received trial-by-trial feedback; receivers could obtain significant results when the biased source did not produce significant chi-squares. However, if chi-square values were found not to indicate bias in a comparatively long sequence then a mathematical inference strategy would be unlikely to allow the receiver to produce a significant level of scoring.

Coding the output

A further point is relevant to the choice of what output to test, regardless of whether global or local tests are used. Palmer and

Weiner (1985) recommend that experimenters using the RAND Corporation (1955) tables to order Zener symbols (circle, cross, wavy lines, square, star) as targets for ESP studies should stick to the traditional coding scheme of 1 and 6 for a circle, 2 and 7 for a cross, and so on rather than using schemes in which low digits are contrasted with high digits (1 and 2 for a circle, 9 and 0 for a star).

This proposal is based on their discovery that the frequency of the digits 1 to 5 slightly but significantly exceeds the frequency of the digits 6 to 0 across the whole table of one million digits (50.13 per cent as opposed to 49.87 per cent, chi-square = 6.87, 1 d.f., $p < .01$). Although their point is specific to this particular case, it implies that experimenters should in general apply randomness tests not to the 'raw' output of an RNG, but to the coded output. Hyman and Honorton (1986) recommend that experimenters should report the rules for translating the RNG's output into target identities, which would make it easy to see whether the coding used in any study would give rise to any problems of this nature.

Choice of randomness tests

Just as the choice of output to test varies, so does the choice of what randomness tests to apply.

Tests of frequency of targets (recommended by, for example, Davis and Akers, 1974) are more common than tests of sequential dependence. Sequential dependency in the target series would affect only the variance and not the mean chance expectation (MCE) in a study where receivers' responses were also sequentially dependent. Some experimenters may assume that as long as MCE is unaffected, there is no problem. However, since a change in either MCE or variance would invalidate the assumptions underlying the usual inferential statistics, this seems a difficult practice to defend in most situations.

Hyman and Honorton (1986) propose that for ganzfeld (and, by implication other) experiments in which only one response is made per session, sequential dependence in the response sequence is unlikely to be an issue and a frequency analysis of targets is therefore sufficient. This might or might not be true in practice, although no data are provided to support the assertion. In principle, however, there are a number of opportunities for sequential dependence between calls in typical ganzfeld designs that might make sequential dependence in the target series a problem. When receivers take part

in more than one trial in a ganzfeld study there may well be dependence between their calls, even if the trials are a day or more apart (as is usual in ganzfeld studies); a receiver may be reluctant to choose a target in the same position in the judging set as on the previous trial. Studies in which receivers carry out only one trial each are common in free-response ESP research but even here sequential dependence between the calls of receivers is possible. In some experiments, an experimenter who is blind to the target's identity helps the receiver through the judging process and could unconsciously influence the receiver to avoid choosing a target in the same position in the set as the previous receiver's choice. If independent judges were instead used to determine the call for each trial and were given the trials to judge in the same order as they were conducted, the judges' choices might show sequential dependence. The only situation in which sequential dependence of responses could be clearly ruled out is the special case in which each receiver takes part in only one trial per study, without being aware of other receivers' calls on previous trials, and either judges alone or has his or her call chosen by a judge who is judging trials in a randomised sequence.

Although some experimenters do report sequential dependency tests for target sequences, most who do so examine only the dependency between adjacent digits (lag 1). There appears to be little agreement between commentators on how far sequential dependency tests should go in terms of digit lag. Palmer (1989) suggests that the issue in ESP research is not whether a target sequence is perfectly random (since no RNG can be so) but whether the sequence is unpredictable given the cognitive capacities of the receiver. Research on subjective random generation (SRG) examines non-randomness in the sequences of digits or symbols that people produce when asked to create a random series. This area of inquiry might be expected to give some idea of the lag at which people's memories fail to allow them to be non-random, despite themselves. Unfortunately, few SRG experiments have analysed call sequences beyond lag 2 and, when higher-order dependencies have been examined, measures that mix all orders have been used (Wagenaar, 1972). Wagenaar suggests that the appropriate lag might be expected to depend on several factors including the number of target alternatives, the extent to which target alternatives lend themselves to a natural ordering, the length of the sequence produced (because of boredom effects), the mode of response (verbal, written, or motor), whether the target choices remain visually displayed during the test, the response rates and individual differences.

Side-stepping such complexity, Tart and Dronek (1982) pragmatically point out that although there are mathematical or memory prodigies who have unusual abilities with numbers, most people's memory capacity for digits is probably less than ten, making that a reasonable upper limit. Davis and Akers (1974), writing at a time when computers were less widely available than they are now, recommended lag 1 tests as a minimum, preferring tests up to lag 6 if a computer was available. Palmer (1986b) suggests that slight degrees of non-randomness beyond the first order of dependence are unlikely to be a serious problem. However, he points out that tests to a greater depth might be appropriate in studies where receivers each take part in a lengthy series of trials and receive trial-by-trial feedback which might allow them to detect and exploit higher-order dependencies than they would generate naturally.

There are many possible tests for sequential dependence (Radin, 1985). The most common in parapsychology involve testing the frequency of occurrence of each possible pairing of targets across various separations in position, or of the occurrence of each possible digram, trigram and so on but we are aware of no specific recommendations concerning what test or tests of sequential dependence should be preferred for ESP research.

Reporting of randomness tests

Davis and Akers (1974) recommend that randomness tests should be routinely included in ESP studies wherever possible with the results of control tests for non-deterministic RNGs reported alongside the experimental results.

Chapter 5 Type of participant

Researchers have to decide whether they wish to work with 'special' participants (i.e. those claiming strong ESP abilities), 'selected' participants (i.e. those who have passed some form of initial screening) or 'unselected' participants. The choice of participant influences the degree to which researchers are expected to guard against cheating and the amount of participant information that should be contained in an experimental report. The following sections discuss these issues.

Extent of experimental safeguards against cheating
Although some commentators propose the most stringent controls for all studies (e.g. Hansel, 1966; Rhine, 1938), most believe that whereas studies using unselected participants should guard against opportunistic cheating (e.g. Hansen, 1990), far more extensive precautions should be taken in studies involving selected and special participants, particularly when only one or two participants take part in the study (e.g. Akers, 1984; Hansen, 1990).

Skilled or planned cheating on the part of highly motivated participants is far more difficult to rule out or detect than might be expected by those unfamiliar with such problems. General strategies, as opposed to specific safeguards against trickery are beyond the scope of the present review but we strongly recommend three texts by Hansen (1990), Morris (1986a) and Wiseman and Morris (1995) on this topic. They propose that researchers educate themselves generally about fraud and trickery and consider consulting with appropriately experienced magicians about their laboratory procedures, especially if they are developing new methods or are dealing with special participants.

Participant information

Reports of studies using unselected participants are not usually expected to contain information relevant to assessing how likely they are to be fraudulent, although Hyman (1985) suggests that researchers should report what proportion of sender-receiver pairs in telepathy studies are friends, since friends might be more likely to collude. More information is required for studies using selected participants, however. Hansen (1990) recommends that reports of studies with an allegedly gifted participant should include a statement describing his or her background, if any, in using trickery, including previous suspicious behaviour even if trickery was not proven. Wiseman and Morris (1995) recommend for this purpose a literature search for previous experimentation with the claimant, as well as informal discussion with researchers who carry out testing of special claimants in case useful information has not made its way into print.

Hansen also requires the reporting of suspicious behaviour during the researcher's own experiment and the Parapsychological Association's (1980) ethical guidelines recommend that researchers make public any clear evidence of cheating in their studies in the case of a participant widely known for making claims of psi ability. If a participant has made public claims of psi abilities, Hansen suggests that this information should also be included in the experimental report along with the participant's name. He also recommends that if there are published accounts of the participant's alleged psychic feats, these should be cited in case they contain details that might suggest trickery to a magician. He would require less stringent reporting requirements for studies with several participants, rather than those with a single special participant, but nevertheless recommends giving individual results for each participant (as also suggested by Hyman and Honorton, 1986), especially if the validity of a study's conclusions depended upon a few participants' results. In this way, readers who thought cheating a possibility could eliminate one or more high scorers (with a justification of the percentage excluded) and reassess the results.

Wiseman and Morris (1995) recommend that, when testing special claimants, researchers should try to assess whether the claimant has any special abilities that might help him or her to cheat successfully. They suggest that researchers should ask the claimant whether he or she belongs to any magicians' organisations and, given that a claimant intending to cheat may not be honest, should also themselves check the membership lists of magicians' organisations at a local, national and international level. They also recommend attempting to discover whether the claimant has any informal contacts with the magical community (a step also recommended by Hansen, 1990). An anonymous respondent in Milton's (1996) questionnaire survey points out that experimenters should not rely upon the claimant for accurate details about any details of his or her background or history, including his or her real name.

As another means of assisting readers to assess the likelihood that special claimants might have attempted to cheat, Wiseman and Morris further propose that researchers should give details of the initial claim and of what modifications were made to that claim during any pilot testing. They also recommend reporting any deviations from intended procedure in any test since such information might alert those with a knowledge of magic to attempts on the claimant's part to negotiate safeguards away. Weiner (1995) further suggests that details should be reported of any agreement drawn up between experimenter and claimant concerning what use the claimant can make of the study's results. It might be expected that if a claimant is free to use positive results for self-advertisement this might act as a powerful incentive to cheat.

Some commentators require details about experimenters as well as about participants. For studies with special participants Hansen (1990) suggests that experimenters report details of their own background (or lack of one) in conjuring and of their ability to make the crucial observations. Although such information is valuable, Wiseman and Morris (1995) additionally recommend the use of videotaping and other media (stills photography, drawings, etc.) so that people who later wish to assess the study need not rely entirely upon the experimenters' powers of observation and memory, even if the experimenter is a skilled observer.

Chapter 6 Sensory shielding I: Pre-trial safeguards

It is obviously vital that receivers should not be able to gain any information about the target via normal sensory channels during an experiment. This chapter discusses what sources of information need to be shielded from the receiver before the trial takes place and how to achieve the necessary security.

Safeguards before target selection

Even before the targets for an experiment are selected it can be possible for dishonest participants to cheat if they can either influence a non-deterministic target selection process or discover enough details about a deterministic one. Wiseman, Beloff and Morris (1992) point out that access to mechanical or electronic RNGs prior to the experiment must be prevented in case participants might be able to bias them in favour of producing a target or target sequence that the receiver intends to call. Morgan (1987) describes a number of ways in which participants with access to a target-generating computer could tamper with it. He suggests methods for detecting and preventing such tampering but lack of access is clearly the simplest and cheapest safeguard. There are some laboratories that use deterministic randomisation sources such as random number tables and pseudo-RNGs and that both publish their randomisation procedure in detail and use the same procedure in more than one study. We suggest that they should not use information that the participants have access to (such as newspaper weather tables or the participant's birthdate) in order to deterministically select seed numbers or entry points. Otherwise there is a risk that participants could calculate what the targets for their trials would be. Wiseman, Beloff and Morris (1992), when testing their special claimant, purposely gave out no advance information about their randomisation method and used a non-deterministic procedure to avoid this problem.

Safeguards during target selection
Most commentators agree that the shielding of the experiment's chosen targets should be in place at the time when target selection takes place in case a participant might attempt some form of covert monitoring of the target selection procedure. Wiseman, Beloff and Morris (1992), for example, ensured that the target randomisers were alone when they made the target list for their study.

Safeguards after target selection
The target selection process produces more than just targets that need to be screened from receivers. After target selection has taken place, there are materials that could help identify the targets. Also, certain laboratory personnel will either know the targets' identities or have been exposed to information that could give them that knowledge.

Shielding target-identifying materials from receivers
Morris (1986b) recommends that any record of the target's identity be kept from participants as completely as the target itself. As well as obvious target records such as target lists, Wiseman, Beloff and Morris (1992) point out that an impression of the randomiser's list on pages of the pad used to record the sequence would also constitute a target record that needs to be protected, destroyed or not created in the first place. In their study they ensured that the target list was not recorded in such a way as to leave an impression on any surface underneath. In free-response experiments in which the target pool is divided into sets, another kind of target record exists: someone could deduce the target's identity by seeing the control items left behind in the set when the target has been removed to be used in the trial. The control items must therefore be stored with appropriate security.

However, the lengths to which experimenters should go to protect their records are unclear. Some special claimants might conceivably be prepared to go to considerable lengths to cheat, perhaps to the point of breaking into a laboratory at night and disassembling and reassembling a filing cabinet to access the target records without detection, for example. In such a case, merely locking target records away in an ordinary piece of furniture in the usual way would be insufficient.

A few experimenters have reported stringent precautions in this regard. Target record security in a study by Delanoy, Watt, Morris and Wiseman (1993) involved locking target records in a metal cabinet whose doors could not be removed without access to the inside. The doors were secured by a conventional key lock and two additional locking systems using tamper-evident, uniquely numbered tags. Also, Wiseman, Beloff and Morris (1992) secured the target list in a special, commercially produced security envelope designed to make undetectable tampering extremely difficult and had the envelope checked immediately before use to determine that no one had previously tampered with its sealing strip in such a way as to make later interference undetectable.

Computer security becomes an issue when target identities or experimental records are stored on computer. Akers (1984) recommends limiting participants' access to the computer. Morgan (1987) lists a number of methods that can be used to prevent access to computer-held information, including the use of optical fibre cables to prevent electromagnetic monitoring of data passing down a computer line (monitoring of optically transmitted information is possible but would require a very complex and obvious monitor), shielding of VDU screens to prevent the computer screen being reconstituted elsewhere and cryptographic methods. His comments are aimed mainly at experimenters dealing with special claimants.

Shielding non-blind laboratory personnel from receivers

It is widely accepted that the receiver should have no contact before or during the trial with any individual (e.g. a sender, experimenter or research assistant) who knows the identity of the target because that individual might inadvertently give away cues to the target's identity (Akers, 1984; Gardner, 1989; Hansel, 1980; Lawrence, 1993; Marks and Kammann, 1980; Milton, 1993, 1994). Some commentators (e.g. Akers, 1984; Stanford and Stein, 1994) also believe that this safeguard should extend to individuals who have prepared targets while attempting to remain blind to them (by shuffling cards without looking at them, for example) because subtle cues may be available to the individual in such circumstances. When each target package contains a different target, Schmeidler points out that no laboratory members who see targets being put into their containers should have contact with the receiver during the trial in case they recognise distinctive marks on the containers and inadvertently cue receivers to the target identity.

In free-response studies it would be easier to communicate some information accidentally about the session's single target than in forced-choice studies with their sequences of targets for each session. In free-response studies, therefore, precautions against even indirect contact between non-blind laboratory personnel and receivers are taken; Honorton (1985) considered ganzfeld studies to be flawed if the senders' experimenter had contact with the receiver's experimenter before the end of the trial. In those studies in which the receiver's experimenter requires the target package during the trial (as when the target package is in the receiver's room for that time), precautions are taken to prevent the receiver's experimenter from meeting or even seeing any intermediary who is needed to pass the target package to the experimenter. Some researchers also try to prevent the experimenter from hearing the intermediary in case of auditory cues or instruct the intermediary to position the target package in the same place each time to avoid position cues.

Chapter 7 Sensory shielding II: Safeguards during the trial

Having dealt with security before the trial, the next stage is to put in place appropriate shielding during the trial itself. Assuming that shielding of target records and non-blind laboratory personnel remains in place, the receiver must now be screened from the targets, from senders (in telepathy studies) and, in some cases, from possible accomplices.

Shielding targets from receivers

A key procedure for target security during the trial itself is the supervision of the receiver by an experimenter and it appears these days to be a given. This may be, at least in part, due to the heavy criticism that J.G. Pratt attracted when he carried out a telepathy experiment with special claimant Hubert Pearce (Rhine and Pratt, 1954). Pearce was left unsupervised in a room in a different building from Pratt, who acted as the sender, and Hansel (1961) suggested that Pearce might have left his room and seen the targets either through the transom above the door into Pratt's room or through a trapdoor in the ceiling. Rhine and Pratt (1961) and, later, Stevenson (1967) attempted to rebut this criticism but not to Hansel's (1980) satisfaction; the potential freedom of action given to Pearce made it difficult to be certain that he could not have cheated.

However, in many cases mere supervision of the receiver is not enough. When the target or target sequence is in the same room as the receiver, for example, additional safeguards are necessary.

Clairvoyance studies with target in same room as receiver
The use of unshielded targets in the same room as the receiver was widely criticised (e.g. Kennedy, 1938; Herbert, 1938). Even partially shielded targets (for example, targets concealed from the receiver by a screen) are not favoured by many commentators because receivers might glimpse the target in a reflective surface such as a window, shiny table-top, someone's spectacles or even corneas (e.g. Hansen, 1980; Morris, 1986b; Schmeidler, 1977) or receive cues from other people in the room who can see the target. If targets are being written down or drawn during the trial (a very unusual procedure) there is a risk that the receiver could decipher the target identities from seeing the pen's movements (Marks and Kammann, 1980; Morris, 1986b) or, especially in the case of forced-choice targets, from hearing the sound of the pen. Blindfolding the receiver under these circumstances is not a solution (e.g. Morris, 1986b) because there are many ways of circumventing blindfolds.

Target shielding, therefore, is generally achieved these days by enclosing targets in opaque containers when they are in the same room as the receiver, as recommended by Akers (1984), Morris (1978) and Schmeidler (1977). Akers also suggests that the opacity of the container should be objectively assessed; details of the container's materials and construction would also be helpful in assessing both its opacity and its resistance to tampering. If the same container is to contain the same target in a later trial with the same receiver, the receiver or an accomplice could place visual or tactile marks on the container so that the receiver would recognise it and know the target identity (Gardner, 1989; Hansen, 1990). The receiver could also recognise distinguishing marks that already happened to be on the container such as wrinkles in an envelope or flecks or irregularities in a cardboard container. Gardner (1989) suggests that both of these methods might have been possible in tests with special participant Pavel Stepanek and suggests that they could have been ruled out by preventing Stepanek from touching or seeing the target containers.

Clairvoyance studies with target within receiver's reach
In a minority of studies, usually those involving special participants, the target container is within easy reach of the receiver or even in the receiver's hands. Under such circumstances, Akers recommends that the container must be rendered fraudproof. Hansen (1990) points out that envelopes offer little security. As Morris (1986b) notes, 'opaque'

paper envelopes can be rendered transparent by applying alcohol, which evaporates quickly leaving no trace. Water or oil can also render paper transparent and any fluid could be applied unobtrusively to an envelope by, for example, being fed from a small vial through a tube to a flesh-coloured sponge attached to the receiver's hand (Morris, 1986b). Shining a bright point light source immediately behind an envelope can also reveal its contents (Morris, 1978, 1986b).

Some studies have been criticised because target containers that were within the receiver's reach have been either left unsealed (Akers, 1984; Gardner, 1989; Milton, 1993) or been sealed in such a way that tampering with the seal might not have been detected. Hansen (1990), discussing research with special claimants, suggests that secret markings could be made at envelope seams or other locations to help in the detection of tampering. Delanoy et al. (1993) took care to use commercially produced bags designed to make undetectable tampering extremely difficult, as did Wiseman, Beloff and Morris (1992), although in these unusual studies the target containers were chosen for situations in which receivers were not supervised by experimenters during the trial. However, in both studies, the experimenters carefully examined target containers for signs of tampering after the receiver's response had been secured and then opened the package themselves, procedures that make sense whenever target security depends heavily on container sealing.

Apart from tampering with a container's seal, another potential problem is the substitution of a near-identical container that holds a target that the receiver intends to call or that replaces a container that the receiver has detectably broken into. Some commentators suggest that target containers should bear secret marks or codes to prevent this problem (Akers, 1984) although independent records of the target's identity are another, perhaps easier, option.

Cues may be available from the target package even without tampering with or switching a container. Free-response targets often differ from each other in weight, size and other physical characteristics that the receiver might discern by handling the target container and use to identify the target by normal means. In a study in which participants took target packages home with them, Delanoy et al. (1993) attempted to avoid such problems by mounting their pictorial free-response targets onto cards of standard size, placing them in jiffy bags to prevent the edges or thickness of the targets being apparent and adding extra paper to packages when necessary so that each target package weighed within one gram of all the others. Such attention to making the contents of target packages indistinguishable from the outside would appear to be valuable when packages are to be handled and the physical characteristics of targets differ within a set.

Shielding senders from receivers

The use of a telepathy design introduces problems of shielding the receiver from any target-related cues that the sender might give, unintentionally or otherwise. Possible unintentional cues include subvocal whispering of the name of the target, and body movements, breathing patterns, facial expressions and so on that might be associated with one target alternative rather than another.

To test the effectiveness of such cues, Schmeidler and Lindemann (1966) deliberately introduced some rather obvious cues in a forced-choice ESP test by having the sender stand in front of the receivers and hold the targets in different ways according to the target identities. Most of the receivers were unaware of the cues but, as Schmeidler and Lindemann point out, any experiment might contain more observant participants or might have factors that would make such cues more salient to most participants. To rule out unintentional cueing by senders and the easier forms of cheating, these days the receiver and sender are normally in different rooms during the trial, as recommended by Akers (1984), Lawrence (1993) and Stanford and Stein (1994). Schmeidler (1977) considers that an insulated wall or one with an air space is necessary between the receiver's and sender's rooms, rather than an ordinary single wall, and Milton (1993) awarded meta-analytic quality credit only to studies with at least one room between sender and receiver or in which the sender was in a commercial or tested sound-attenuated chamber.

Supervision of both receiver and sender is also generally recommended. For ganzfeld studies, Hyman and Honorton (1986) consider that a two-experimenter design in which receiver and sender are each supervised by their own experimenter effectively rules out sensory leakage during the trial; Hyman (1985) awarded meta-analytic credit only to studies with this two-experimenter design. Milton (1993) assigned credit to telepathy studies in which both sender and receiver were supervised by an experimenter either jointly or individually and Lawrence (1993) awarded credit for vigilant monitoring of sender and receiver.

However, simple separation and supervision of participants may not be enough, especially if the experimenter might not know what observations of the sender might be crucial to detect deception. For example, changes in lighting conditions could be used by the sender to signal to the receiver, as was the case in a study by Estabrooks (1947; see also Nicol, 1976). Even a supervised sender might use his or her shadow against a crack under the door in the receiver's line of sight as a signal, disguising his or her movements as natural body movements, and an experimenter not alert to this form of trickery might not be aware of what was going on. This scenario suggests the importance of visual screening between the sender's room and that of the receiver so that the supervising experimenter does not need to be relied upon to detect subtle cues.

Auditory or vibrational cues are another potential problem. Akers (1984) recommends tests of auditory transmission between the receiver's and sender's rooms. Instrumented testing is rare, although Dalton et al. (1994) describe such tests carried out at the Koestler Chair of Parapsychology's facilities at Edinburgh University. The tests covered the human auditory spectrum, which seems wise given that Hansel (1959, 1980) and Scott and Goldney (1960) have suggested that senders might use high pitched whistles to cheat. Informal tests in which laboratory personnel in the receiver's room attempt to detect someone shouting or jumping up and down in the sender's room are not unusual in experimental reports, however, and details of the physical structures separating sender and receiver are also often given so that readers can assess how likely sound and vibration is to carry through the building. Hansel (1980), discussing the research with a special subject at SRI, pointed out that a ventilation system has the potential to be a channel for auditory signals and that the sound created by a system itself could be modulated by blocking and unblocking the outlet. We have never seen any mention of heating pipes in connection with auditory signalling but since they can easily carry sound between rooms it may be advisable to describe what circumstances or procedures would prevent a sender from using heating pipes to communicate with the receiver.

The use of radio waves, by means of miniaturised radio transmitters and receivers, provides another possible means of cheating (Akers, 1984; Hanlon, 1974; Hansen, 1990; Morris, 1986b;

Soal and Bowden, 1960; Targ and Puthoff, 1974; Wiseman and Morris, 1995). As Hansen points out, these devices can be inconspicuous and Akers asserts that they are regularly used by some students for classroom cheating. Faraday cages, which are earthed wire mesh cages that attenuate reception of radiowaves inside them, are rarely used in ESP studies although newly built laboratories may have them designed in (e.g., Dalton et al., 1994). However, even Faraday cages are not completely effective, particularly at the low frequency end of the electromagnetic range.

Hansen suggests that when security is especially crucial, a laboratory member could be the sender, rather than someone who might collude with the receiver. Wiseman and Morris suggest using commercially available electronic counter-surveillance apparatus when the use of transmitters is a serious possibility. Whatever the type of cue under consideration - visual, auditory or electromagnetic - Akers (1984) points out that the effectiveness of the shielding against it must be assessed at the time of the experiment in case it has been weakened by modifications such as the introduction of cable holes in walls.

Finally, timing cues are a concern in studies in which the sender, or the sender's experimenter, signals to the receiver and his or her experimenter that the sender is ready to begin the trial although such studies are increasingly rare. Senders and receivers who are colluding to cheat could easily use timing codes to inform the receiver of the target's identity by variations in time gaps between signals (Annemann, 1938; Morris, 1978), the length of the signal (Morris, 1978), the time at which the signal occurs (Hansel, 1990) and so on. Inadvertent cueing is possible if the time taken for the sender to become ready is somehow related to the target's identity or content. For example, video clips might be used in a free-response study and the sender's preparation time might be related to the amount of time taken to wind back the video machine to the target clip, thus alerting the receiver to its position within the judging set (Morris et al., 1993). Even if the receiver did not pick up on such cues, the receiver's experimenter, having greater familiarity with the situation, might become subconsciously aware of them and bias the receiver in favour of the target clip.

Targets that need different amounts of preparation on the spot, such as drawings made at the beginning of the trial, might also provide time cues and are inadvisable for other reasons (see the section on free-response judging problems later). Akers (1984) recommends that if 'ready' signals are necessary in an experiment they should operate only from the receiver's room to the sender's room. Schmeidler (1977) agrees and suggests automatic signalling or signalling by a blind experimenter as other acceptable options.

Discussing free-response telepathy studies in which the experimenter supervised the receiver from another room, Wiseman, Smith and Kornbrot (1996) point out that the receiver's experimenter as well as the receiver must be adequately shielded from the sender and target. Otherwise, the experimenter might unconsciously pick up cues and pass them on to the receiver during the judging process. This concern applies to all studies in which the experimenter might influence the receiver's response.

Shielding accomplices from receivers

An accomplice can help the receiver to cheat by accessing the target either directly, or via a colluding sender, and passing information about the target to the receiver. Marks and Kammann (1980) criticised Targ and Puthoff (1974) for allowing friends of a spacial subject to be present in the laboratory during his trials. Hansen (1990) recommends that researchers report who was present during testing with special claimants. (It should be noted that it is very rare that anyone other than laboratory personnel are with the receiver during a trial.)

Experimenters do not often directly address in their reports what safeguards, if any, were taken against possible accomplices but the emphasis generally appears to be on preventing an accomplice from accessing the target rather than from passing information to the receiver. Hansel (1966, 1980) criticised Pratt's experiment with special participant Hubert Pearce (Rhine and Pratt, 1954) because the target was on display in a room that he considered inadequately visually screened. Marks and Kammann (1990) pointed out that the soundproof chamber in which Targ and Puthoff's (1974) a special subject was situated was not as good a screen as it appeared because a cable hole in the wall of the chamber was blocked only by some removable wadding. If receivers might be supposed to cheat in these ways, the implication is that an accomplice might be equally ready to interfere with a building's structure or find an unsupervised weak point in a room's shielding to peek into a room containing an unscreened target.

Chapter 8 Sensory shielding III: Post-trial safeguards

Issues of target shielding continue to be important right up to the point at which the response records have been secured. Security of experimental records remains an issue after the experiment itself is completed. This chapter discusses the relevant precautions.

Post-trial target shielding

Akers (1984) and Morris (1986b) point out that safeguards taken to shield the target and target records from the receiver should continue until after the response records have been secured. This is important because if receivers learn or are told what the target or target sequence was after the session is over, they might attempt to alter their response records to match it. Marks and Kammann (1980) suggested that the design of Targ and Puthoff's (1974) study would have allowed cheating in this way. Especially in forced-choice experiments it might occur even to unselected participants to alter the record of their responses if it is still in their possession when they get target feedback since it would be easy to change some symbols to others relatively undetectably. Some participants might not even realise that their behaviour would be considered wrong by the experimenter; they might remember thinking of the actual target at the time they made their call and persuade themselves that the target is a better representation of what they were thinking on that trial than the call they actually made. This problem of altering responses to fit the target feedback can be avoided if the experimenter secures the record of the receiver's response before feedback and allows no additions or alterations to it thereafter (Akers, 1984, Morris, 1986b).

In telepathy studies, the sender often joins the receiver and receiver's experimenter after the response period is over to show them what the target or target sequence was, and to learn what the receiver's guess was. Hyman (1985) and Hyman and Honorton (1986) recommend that measures should be taken to prevent a sender substituting a target at that time to match the receiver's response (Hyman, 1985; Hyman and Honorton, 1986). In most studies this would be difficult: in free-response experiments senders generally are only given access to the target for the trial and not to any of the control items in the set and in forced-choice studies senders do not have prior access to laboratory record sheets. However, where there is potential for such a problem it could be avoided by double-checking the target in the sender's possession against the laboratory records of what the targets ought to be. Morris (1986b) recommends treating the target record as though it were the target itself to circumvent substitution attempts by either the sender or receiver.

Post-trial target record shielding

Even after the response has been secured, some security for experimental records may be necessary. Wiseman, Beloff and Morris (1992) took steps to prevent undetectable post-trial tampering with the response list by copying it and storing the copies in different locations; such duplication of target and response records is recommended by Morris (1986b). Schmeidler (1994) suggests that all experimental records be made in indelible ink, which would add an additional layer of security. The discussion of what level of pre-trial security was necessary for target records also applies here.

Chapter 9 Free-response judging

Free-response designs have become popular for ESP studies since the early 1960s. Although each trial takes much longer to conduct, free-response studies are associated with much higher effect sizes per trial than forced-choice studies. There are, however, a number of pitfalls to be avoided in free-response studies, some of them rather subtle.

Blind transcription, transcription checking, response handling and judging

First, it is often necessary to have the receiver's mentation transcribed, as when the receiver makes a verbal mentation report, and the receiver or independent judge will need a written record of it for the judging process. In order to avoid cues, transcription is commonly done by someone who is blind to the target's identity. Similarly, any checking of the transcript with the original for accuracy (against the receiver's memory, against the audiotape of the receiver's mentation report or against the original of a mentation report that has been translated into a foreign language, for example) would also need to be done by someone blind to the target's identity. To maintain the blind, it also follows that the judge should have little or no contact with anyone who knows the target identity for any trial and that instructions to judges should be given or written by someone who is blind to the target identities; although some authors give details of how judges are kept blind, most do not. In addition, we recommend that neither participants nor experimenters who know the target identity should handle the receiver's response sheet, or the transcription of it, before the judge sees it. Otherwise, deliberate or accidental alterations, marks, creases, smudges and so on might draw the judge's attention to the target-related sections.

Handling cues

A number of authors (e.g. Akers, 1984; Hyman, 1977a, 1985; Kennedy, 1979a; Sargent, 1980; Stokes, 1978) have criticised open-deck telepathy studies for giving the judge (whether the receiver or an independent judge) a judging set that included the target that was handled by an experimenter or by the sender in a telepathy study. Handling would raise the possibility that the judge could identify the target because it alone would show handling cues such as fingerprints, traces of perfume, residual heat (and fading in the case of a projector slide) or even marks placed on the target deliberately by the sender.

In direct experimental tests of whether unselected participants would or could use such cues, Palmer (1983) compared the ability of a group of receivers to select the target from a set that included the target handled by the sender with that of a group of receivers who only saw a duplicate set. No significant difference was found but Palmer and Kramer (1986), by explicitly instructing participants to select from a set of four photographs the one that showed most evidence of handling, found that 45 per cent of them were able to do so. These findings suggest that, although unselected participants might not pay attention to handling cues without prompting, it is nevertheless possible to exploit such cues.

Palmer and Kramer recommended that no journal should accept a free-response ESP paper that did not include some precaution to rule out the possibility of handling cues. These days, in free-response studies that require judging sets, duplicate sets rather than single sets are used as recommended by Akers (1984), Honorton (1985), Hyman (1985), Hyman and Honorton (1986), Kennedy (1979a), Milton (1993), Palmer (1986a) and Sargent (1980). We have seen no discussion of this problem with respect to closed-deck studies, perhaps because all targets in the judging set would be expected to show unintentional handling cues to an equal degree. However, if the same sender and receiver pair did several trials in a study and the receiver was the judge, they could cheat by having the sender mark targets with some pre-arranged code. As before, duplicate sets would be a solution to this. However, closed-deck studies often use targets that have no duplicates such as unique objects; in such a case, preventing the sender from handling the targets would be one way of avoiding cues. Alternatively, or in cases when handling cannot be ruled out (e.g. if targets are geographical sites, where the sender could unobtrusively leave markers) independent judging rather than receiver judging should be used.

Cues from contemporaneous target description

Another potential sensory cueing problem can arise in the case of closed-deck studies that use targets whose qualities change with time and circumstance, such as geographical locations or people. Judges are usually given descriptions of the target sets in these cases, rather than being taken to the target set locations or meeting the target people themselves. If these descriptions are made contemporaneously with the trial, it may be possible to match the target with the transcript by extraneous cues alone. For example, if it is raining at the time of the trial, the receiver's mentation transcript may include references to rain. A contemporaneous written description of a geographical target might also mention rain or that the streets were wet and so on. Photographs would clearly show the weather conditions. A description of a human target on a rainy day might include references to waterproof clothing and wet hair.

To avoid such cues, Kennedy (1979a) recommended that descriptions of the target pool should be prepared in advance of the experiment. Kennedy's suggested procedure would also circumvent the possibility that an experimenter who knew the contents of the receiver's mentation transcript for a trial might also be the person to describe the target for the judge, inadvertantly emphasising those aspects of the target that matched the transcript. We are aware of no experiment in which this was clearly a strong possibility but Marks and Kammann (1980) offer it as a speculative scenario in their critique of Targ and Puthoff's remote viewing work.

Ordering of items within the judging set

Other cues to the judge may be available if the judging set is not presented to him or her in random order. Before duplicate sets were commonly used, in some studies using pictures as targets, the target was simply shuffled back in with the control pictures in the set before being presented to the judge. With such a method, targets may have tended to end up in the same position more often than chance and any tendency on the judge's part to choose pictures in a particular position as the target would have resulted in a deviation from the expected theoretical variance in outcomes, invalidating the statistical test used to test the null hypothesis. Honorton (1985), Hyman (1985) and Milton (1993) required that the position of the target in the target set be random when presented to the judge for their meta-analytic quality criterion for open-deck studies.

For closed-deck studies, Kennedy (1979b), Marks and Kammann (1978, 1980), Milton (1993) and Palmer (1986a) recommended that each trial's target should be presented in random order with respect to the order of presentation of each trial's mentation transcript in case cues in the receivers' transcripts allowed them to be placed in temporal order (or even approximate order) by the judge. For example, Marks and Kammann suggested that in a study with a single receiver, the receiver might make references to mentation from previous trials or targets that would allow the judge to order the transcripts, or the transcripts might get shorter in later trials as the receiver became more practised or got bored more quickly. Gardner (1981) suggests that if transcripts are typed, the type might get fainter and the typist might make more mistakes for the later transcripts, also providing order cues. It should be noted that in some closed-deck studies randomisation of the target order within the judging set may not be enough. Akers (1984), Kennedy (1979a) and Marks and Kammann (1978, 1980) all recommend that judges should not know or be able to deduce the order in which targets were presented, as might happen if the judge was the sender or if contemporaneous descriptions of targets that change over time are being used or if the experimenters provide the judge with target order information.

In many open-deck studies there is no need to randomise the position of the target in the judging set because the items are always fixed in the same order regardless of which is the target. For both open-deck and closed-deck studies for which this is not the case, relatively informal methods of randomisation are sometimes used to determine the position of the target within the set for presentation to the judge. Given that it is just as easy to use extensively tested randomness sources for this purpose, these more formal methods are to be recommended.

Cues from length of target presentation
In some free-response experiments, such as those using movie clips or pieces of music as targets, targets within a judging set differ in length of presentation. In such cases, it is not always made clear that the receiver's response period is always of a fixed length, rather than being determined by the length of target presentation. In the latter situation, the length of the mentation transcript, or receivers' comments about the length of the response period could cue judges to the target identity. Even if response periods were fixed, receivers who were aware of target presentation lengths might also provide cues to judges by directly mentioning presentation length or by some more subtle means such as by differences in the length of, or amount of detail in their transcript and so on. If variable-length targets are being used, therefore, response periods should be fixed and receivers should remain blind to presentation length.

Cues due to feedback
A number of commentators have pointed out that, in closed-deck studies in which receivers receive trial-by-trial feedback and each do several trials, receivers might mention, in any single trial's mentation report, details of targets on previous trials that would tell the independent judge that those targets were not the target for the current trial (Kennedy, 1979b; Marks and Kammann, 1978, 1980).

Some experimenters have tried to overcome the problem by editing the transcript but this editing can give rise to other difficulties. If the editor is not blind to what the target was for a given trial, he or she might inadvertantly edit the trial's transcript in such a way as to enhance the likelihood that the judge will correctly match it to its target (Marks, 1981). An editor who is blind to the contents of the target pool risks leaving in relevant target information if the receiver does not explicitly state that it refers to a target from an earlier trial. An editor who knows what the target pool is, but not what the target was for each transcript, also runs this risk and the additional risk of excising ESP-related mentation if he or she adopts the strategy of removing all mentations that relate to the target pool whether the receiver identifies them as referring to earlier trials' mentations or not. An editor who knows both the target pool and the identity of the target for a given transcript must make non-blind judgements about how to alter the transcript. This raises the possibility, if there is a judgement to be made about ambiguous mentations, of unintentional bias towards leaving in those relevant to the present trial's target.

All three situations have the potential for mistakes and oversights on the editor's part. Also, as pointed out by Akers (1984), Hansel (1980), Hyman (1977b), Kennedy (1979b), Milton (1993) and Palmer (1986a), receivers might tend to avoid mentioning mentation that they know has some correspondence to a previous trial and any surprisingly absent mentations might again indicate to the independent judge that the missing mentations relate to a target that was not the target for that trial. For example, if the receiver usually always mentions the presence of people but does not do so in a number of trials, this might indicate that people had been a feature of an earlier target in the series. Kennedy (1979b), Akers (1984) and Palmer (1986a) recommend that free-response studies should not use closed-deck procedures if trial-by-trial feedback is given and if receivers in the study do more than one trial; they regard the problem as insoluble by editing. It should be noted that if the receiver's experimenter knows what targets from a closed deck have been used in earlier trials in the study, even if the receiver receives no feedback, the experimenter might inadvertently guide the receiver's mentation away from the content of those earlier targets, artificially raising the effect size. Thus, the receiver's experimenter should also receive no feedback of target identities until after response records for the whole study have been secured.

Kennedy (1979b) recommends that if experimenters wish to give receivers trial-by-trial feedback in a free-response study, they should use an open-deck procedure, using unedited transcripts with the judges judging transcripts one at a time in the order in which they were produced, and with the judges prevented from altering their judgements after seeing later responses. In this way, if a receiver made reference to the target on an earlier trial in the transcript of a later trial, the judge could not exploit that information. Without such precautions in open-deck studies, if, for example, a receiver mentioned a frog in one trial's transcript because a frog had been in the target in an earlier trial, and the judge later encountered the target set containing the frog picture, he or she might be more inclined to choose it as the target, resulting in artificially inflated scoring. Even though that target set might be used several times in a single experiment (in open-deck studies, target sets are often used with replacement) it might not be used often enough with a different item in it as the target to overcome this cueing problem. This danger does not only arise in studies in which receivers each do more than one trial but also in those where they do only one trial each but might discuss the experiment with other receivers from the same study. Milton (1993) withheld meta-analytic quality credit from trial-by-trial feedback, open-deck studies in which independent judges judged unedited transcripts out of their original order. This issue of cues in open-deck studies from past transcripts is not one that is often addressed in published studies, possibly because experimenters trust many of their judges to work without such controls; judges are often laboratory personnel or experimenters from other laboratories.

As Kennedy (1979b) points out, the common practice in open-deck studies of having the receiver judge each trial at the end of the response period without using an independent judge rules out the problem of past-transcript cues to the judges in open-deck studies. However, some as yet unpublished analyses of a database of free-response studies (Milton, 1993) have indicated that those studies that used independent judges obtained effect sizes almost five times as large as those using receiver judges. The finding was statistically significant but it is not clear whether it might be an artefact of multiple analysis or of being confounded with some other variables that significantly related to effect size, including one related to a procedural flaw. The first author will soon be carrying out a more focused meta-analysis to address this issue. In the meantime experimenters should be aware that receiver judging may not be the optimum way to avoid the problem of cueing judges from an effect-size point of view although it is certainly the easiest.

Chapter 10 Recording, checking, scoring and calculation procedures

It has long been known that scientists' observations are sometimes in error, a fact first noted by astronomers at the end of the eighteenth century (Boring, 1950). The possibility that observational errors might occur frequently enough to account for the positive results of ESP experiments was considered very early in the literature. Errors can arise in ESP experiments in the transcription of targets produced by random number tables or generators, in the recording of the identities of targets and responses, in the scoring of the number of hits, in data entry into tables for computation and in the experimenter's statistical calculations.

Target transcription errors

A problem that we have not seen discussed in the literature is one that could occur when the randomiser is transcribing a target sequence from a random number generator or random number table. If the randomiser tends to make errors in recording that match receivers' call biases (e.g. recording more of a popular target choice than other targets, avoiding target repetitions and so on), then the assumptions underlying the application of the usual statistical tests to the receivers' scores will not hold. In the absence of automated target transcription, checking is recommended.

Target and response recording

Kennedy and Uphoff (1939) reported three telepathy studies examining the frequency and nature of target and response recording errors under the conditions then prevalent in card-guessing studies, when participants themselves frequently recorded targets and responses. In the first study, psychology students, acting as experimenters or participants in three series of calls, made errors on between 0.7 per cent of trials in the first series and 1.8 per cent in the third. While many errors had no effect on the scores, there was a particularly strong bias in the first series for the remaining errors to raise the score rather than lower it (87 per cent of such errors), although this trend was reversed in the second study (37 per cent of such errors). In a second study, a strong believer in telepathy acted as sender and recorder of the receiver's calls and made errors whose net effect was to raise the number of hits by 46 in the first 1,000 calls.

Kennedy and Uphoff next performed a study to compare the errors made by two groups of psychology students, chosen for extreme belief and disbelief in telepathy respectively, who acted as senders and as recorders of calls and targets. They made errors on 1.1 per cent of trials. Interestingly, both 'believers' and 'disbelievers' made more errors that increased the score than errors that decreased it although the effect was much stronger for the believers; ignoring the errors that had no effect on the score, 80 per cent of the believers' errors increased the score as opposed to 54 per cent of the disbelievers' errors. Kennedy and Uphoff attributed the predomination of score-increasing errors on even the disbelievers' part as being due to the nature of the task, which required the sender to hold the target in mind while recording the receiver's response. Kennedy and Uphoff found that most errors (56 per cent) that decreased the score were due to recorders failing to notice hits. Dale (1943) noted that all recording errors in a clairvoyance card-guessing study that she conducted were of this type. It is also interesting to note that in Kennedy and Uphoff's study there were considerable individual differences between recorders in the percentage of trials on which they made errors with a range from 0.009 per cent to 4 per cent.

A later survey by Rosenthal (1978) found similar results to Kennedy and Uphoff's, in that in twenty-one studies that reported error data from various areas of experimental psychology (including the Kennedy and Uphoff paper as the only parapsychological contribution) recording errors were made on about 1 per cent of trials. However, he also found that the errors tended to favour the observer's hypothesis on about two thirds of the trials, in contrast to Kennedy and Uphoff's findings that even extreme disbelievers made errors that tended to raise the hit rate. Curiously, Kennedy and Uphoff, along with Kennedy (in *The ESP Symposium*, 1938) and Akers (1984) summarise Kennedy and Uphoff's finding by stating that the recorders tended to make errors in line with their beliefs with disbelievers making errors that tended to reduce the score. This is clearly incorrect.

Following Kennedy and Uphoff's (1939) experiments and Kennedy's continued insistence that parapsychologists should take steps to rule out recording and scoring errors (e.g. *The ESP Symposium*, 1938; Kennedy, 1939a, 1939b), a number of authors recommended procedures designed to exclude such errors. Kennedy and Uphoff favoured automation (also later recommended by Schmeidler, 1977). Many studies have since adopted automated methods but, as Akers (1984) points out, automated systems are not perfect and he feels that it is critical that they be checked periodically to ensure that they are functioning properly. Such systems were not generally available in the early days of parapsychology, however, and recommendations concerned the deployment of human observers. Current opinion appears to favour a full double-blind procedure in which the target recorder is blind to the calls and the call recorder is blind to the targets. Akers (1984) and Milton (1993) consider studies to be flawed without this safeguard and Schmeidler (1977) describes it as 'essential' (p.136) in the absence of recorded automation. Palmer (1986a) notes that the randomiser who produces the target list must be blind to the receiver's calls in order to implement this double-blind in precognition studies.

Scoring and counting of hits

Concerning the counting of hits, the most general recommendation has been, and is, to have hits marked and totalled by two different people (e.g. *Research Notes*, 1938; Honorton and Ferrari, 1989; Honorton, Ferrari and Bem, 1990; Milton, 1993; Stanford and Stein, 1994) who are preferably blind to each other's scoring (Schmeidler, 1977), although some meta-analysts have used double-checking as the quality criterion without specifying that each check be carried out by a different person (Honorton and Ferrari, 1989; Lawrence, 1993; Milton, 1994). Rosenthal (1978) generally recommends that data recorders be kept blind to relevant hypotheses as far as possible and so, presumably, would support a double-blind procedure. As an alternative when additional personnel are not available, Schmeidler (1994) suggests that the original scorer could perform the checking with the original scoring concealed and after some time has elapsed or the scorer has confused his or her memory by performing a long series of similar tasks.

Data entry for computation

Errors can also occur in transferring data from individual record sheets to raw data summary tables or computer tables that will be used to make statistical calculations. Such errors can involve psychological test results and condition assignments as well as ESP scores (Palmer, 1996). Double-checking, especially carried out by someone other than the person who transferred the data, would address this potential problem.

Checker details

Although in the early literature participants acted as recorders and data checkers in ESP experiments, this was soon warned against (e.g. *Research Notes*, 1938) and is now rare (although it is, of course, perfectly acceptable for a receiver to record his or her own responses as long as he or she is blind to the target and the experimenter secures the response record before feedback). However, data recording and checking is sometimes handled by someone whose background is not described and Hyman and Honorton (1986) have called for experimenters to report details of the training, supervision, and qualifications of student experimenters in the ganzfeld, a recommendation that might well generalise to all personnel who are not qualified researchers but who are responsible for important parts of experimental procedures.

Checking of statistical calculations

Once data has been collected, the final stage of data handling is the performance of statistical calculations upon it. The *Journal of Parapsychology* requires its authors to have their data and statistical analyses independently re-checked before submitting a paper.

Chapter 11 Reporting and retaining data

Just as pre-specification of certain experimental procedures helps to prevent post-hoc data selection, certain reporting recommendations are designed to address the same problem. In addition, retaining experimental details acts as insurance against inaccurate or incomplete reporting. This chapter discusses these issues.

Selective reporting of trials

Any report should include all the trials run during the experiment. Marks and Kammann (1980) suspected that in a free-response study by Targ and Puthoff the experimenters had not given all the receiver's drawings to the judge. Marks and Kammann pointed out that, if this had been so, the experimenters could have selectively rejected drawings that did not match the target, thereby invalidating the judging process. They also cite evidence that not all the receiver's trials had been included in that and other studies, in some cases possibly because they were classified on a post-hoc basis as demonstration rather than experimental trials. If true, this raises the possibility that the experimenters could simply have chosen to include successful trials in the overall outcome analysis and ignored unsuccessful trials. By this means, any study with a chance outcome could be made to appear successful and this would clearly be a serious flaw.

Marks and Kammann (1980) also criticised Targ and Puthoff for apparently including in the overall outcome analysis successful trials that the receiver had 'passed' on and for rejecting those 'pass' trials that were unsuccessful. This would also be a very serious problem because the purpose of pass trials is to allow receivers to exclude certain trials from the experiment before target feedback. Marks and Kammann do not recommend any specific solution to this problem. We have not seen Targ and Puthoff's procedures repeated by other experimenters but recording in writing whether or not a trial is to be considered part of the experiment by someone who is blind to the trial's outcome would be a straightforward solution.

In some studies, it very occasionally happens that experimenters exclude one or more trials from the study while aware of the trials' outcomes because they only become aware after feedback of the target's identity that there is some problem that has invalidated the trial (such as an RNG fault or some important error in procedure). In such cases, reporting the reason for the trials' exclusion and the outcome data from those trials would allow readers to gauge whether the exclusion was justified and to reassess the data if they disagreed.

In some studies, fewer trials are carried out than were planned. This may be because trials have been excluded for the kind of reasons just discussed and not replaced or because the study terminated early due to laboratory closure, difficulties in recruiting participants and so on. Because the experimenter could almost always choose to persevere in running more trials, such stopping must usually be regarded as optional. In such a case, the experimenter should justify the study's shortfall of trials and report how many trials are missing. The experimenter (or reader) then has the option of correcting for the missing trials in the overall outcome measure by assuming that they would have obtained chance scoring (Bem and Honorton, 1994).

Another possibility for data selection arises in studies in which each participant takes part in more than one trial. Kennedy (1979a) and Akers (1984) recommend that in such studies, experimenters should publish the data of any participants who drop out before completing all their trials in case they have dropped out because they were doing poorly; to neglect their data might give the impression that a study was more successful than it actually was.

Selective reporting of studies

Selective reporting of studies with positive outcomes is recognised as a widespread problem within science and many researchers have called for procedures to solve the problem (e.g. Dunn, 1980;

Sommer and Sommer, 1983). Recognising the potential seriousness of this problem for parapsychology, the Parapsychological Association Board (Parapsychological Association, 1975) adopted some years ago a policy against the selective reporting of positive outcomes. The *European Journal of Parapsychology* attempts to address this problem by offering researchers the option of having their papers refereed on the basis of their introduction, methodology and planned data analysis sections only, prior to the experiment being carried out. This form of selection bias does not appear to be a serious problem in parapsychology, at least in recent years. Null results are frequently published; in the database of free-response studies surveyed by Milton (1993), 77 per cent of the published studies reported non-significant main outcome measures.

Retaining data

The American Psychological Association (*Publication manual*, 1994) expects authors who publish in its journals to retain their data (and analyses, instructions and details of procedure) for at least five years after publication so that data can be rechecked if necessary and so that others can attempt accurate replications of the study. This policy has also been adopted by the Parapsychological Association (Stanford, 1990) for papers presented at its annual convention and therefore reported in *Research in Parapsychology*.

Chapter 12 Other considerations

There remain a number of issues that experimenters may wish to consider that do not fall into any of the categories dealt with already but instead apply to experiments as a whole or concern general experimental policy as opposed to specific safeguards. These issues are safeguards against experimenter fraud, the desirability of consulting with magicians over experimental design, the need for a 'non-ESP' control condition and the correct choice and use of statistical tests. We will deal with each briefly in turn.

Experimenter fraud

To keep this project within manageable bounds, we decided not to cover procedures for ruling out experimenter fraud in this survey. Incorporation of such procedures is quite rare and so we also had doubts that experimenters would wish to include such procedures as a matter of course. Although some commentators consider experimenter fraud a strong possibility, especially if an otherwise stringently conducted ESP experiment produces positive results, others consider controls against experimenter fraud unnecessary and paranoia-inducing. For a brief review of the issues involved we recommend Akers (1984, pp.157-159).

Consultation with magicians

As we have already mentioned, Hansen (1990), Morris (1986a), Randi (1985) and Wiseman and Morris (1995) suggest that researchers consider consulting magicians when developing new experimental procedures or when testing someone who has made strong claims of psychic abilities. However, such consultation is not frequently mentioned and we have privately encountered resistance to the idea on the part of some researchers who do not trust magicians or do not consider them competent in a scientific setting. We particularly recommend Hansen's (1990) paper dealing with this issue.

'Non-ESP' control condition

Most parapsychologists have long argued that, as long as target selection is random, theoretical mean chance expectation is an appropriate baseline with which to compare experimental results if one is simply interested in whether participants are scoring more highly in an ESP task than they would by chance. As Utts (1991) recently stated, "parapsychology is one of the few areas where a point null makes some sense" (p.401). However, some critics have argued that some kind of 'non-ESP' control condition is necessary as a baseline. For example, Boring (1966) proposed that such a control condition could consist of having someone who presumably lacks psi ability taking the test, while others such as Calkins (1980) suggested repeating the test in conditions under which they assume psi to be impossible, such as in the absence of a sender. Gilmore (1989) goes as far as to suggest that the laws of classical probability theory may break down when effect sizes are low, making a theoretical baseline inappropriate but this does not appear to be a commonly held view.

As Palmer (1982) points out, a non-ESP condition seems to be an impossibility; there is no way to be sure that someone has no psi ability and parapsychologists have been unable to find any conditions that appear to preclude scoring above the theoretical chance baseline. Precognition studies, let alone clairvoyance studies, appear to produce results reliably above chance (Honorton and Ferrari, 1989), and there is evidence that studies can also be successful when the receivers are not even aware that they are taking part in an ESP test (Palmer, 1978). Palmer (1982) also remarks that the same probability theory that underlies the use of the theoretical chance baseline also underlies the statistical tests that are used to compare the performance of experimental and control groups.

Whereas with most differences of opinion over experimental safeguards we can see both points of view, we find the arguments for non-ESP control conditions weak. Nevertheless, experienced researchers will be aware that when they present their ESP research to audiences unfamiliar with parapsychology, it is very common for those audiences to criticise the lack of a non-ESP control condition. The first author has therefore recommended elsewhere (Milton, 1995b) that researchers who wish to publish their ESP studies outside the specialist parapsychology journals should include a brief note explaining why there is no need for such a control condition and also, perhaps, why no such condition is possible; Palmer's (1982) paper would be useful to cite in this context. In this way, a paper is less likely to be rejected by a referee unfamiliar with parapsychology (such referees are routinely used to review parapsychology papers submitted to non-parapsychology science journals) and the author will pre-empt letters of complaint to the journal if the paper is published.

Statistics

An issue not included in the main text but that needs brief discussion here concerns the correct choice and application of statistical procedures in ESP experiments. There is no debate on this subject: everybody agrees that experimenters should use the correct statistical test in any given situation. However, using incorrect statistics has not been an uncommon thing in ESP experimentation, particularly under two specific circumstances: first, when an experimenter is unfamiliar with conventional parapsychological statistics and second, when an experimenter is using a new experimental design and asks a statistical consultant with no knowledge of parapsychology for help in selecting an appropriate statistical procedure. Our experience, both in seeking statistical advice and in looking at many ESP studies, is that the latter situation can be extremely problematic. We recommend that if experimenters intend to use a non-standard experimental design, they obtain any statistical advice that they need before finalising their study's design and that they ask for that advice from statisticians who have a special interest in parapsychology. There is at present no parapsychological statistical primer aimed at the serious researcher but Palmer's (1986b) chapter is a good place to begin (note the corrections in some incorrectly printed formulae, pointed out in Palmer, 1986c) and those with an advanced understanding of statistics will find Burdick and Kelly's (1977) chapter useful. A number of common statistical errors made in the analysis of ESP experiments and that researchers should avoid are listed in the Appendix.

Conclusion

The length of this manuscript reflects the sheer volume of critical commentary that has been published over the years and the length of the reference list demonstrates the extent to which this commentary has been scattered. We hope that by collecting and summarising this material we have provided a useful service to this field of research.

Although the main purpose of this text is to provide convenient information sources for those who wish to carry out and assess ESP studies, we hope that it will also serve as a stimulus to those who hold different views about what safeguards are appropriate or who see a 'recommendation gap' where some procedural question has not been addressed. By summarising current opinion, the text indicates at what point someone who wants to argue for additional or different safeguards needs to start the discussion.

It is hoped that we will be able to include these differences of opinion, and suggestions, in a future edition of this text.

References

AKERS, C. (1984). Methodological criticisms of parapsychology. In S. Krippner (Ed.), *Advances in parapsychological research 4* (pp.112-164). New York: Plenum Press.

ANNEMANN. (1938, August). Was Prof. J.B. Rhine hoodwinked? *Jinx*, No. 47, 329, 333.

BEM, D.J. and HONORTON, C. (1994). Does psi exist? Replicable evidence for an anomalous process of information transfer. *Psychological Bulletin*, 115, 4-18.

BORING, E.G. (1950). *A history of experimental psychology* (2nd ed.) New York: Appleton-Century-Crofts.

BORING, E.G. (1966). Paranormal phenomena: Evidence, specification, and chance. In C.E.M. Hansel, *ESP: A scientific evaluation*. New York: Scribner.

BUDESCU, D.V. (1987). A Markov model for generation of random binary sequences. *Journal of Experimental Psychology: Human Perception and Performance*, 13, 25-39.

BURDICK, D.S. and KELLY, E.F. (1977). Statistical methods in parapsychological research. In B.B. Wolman (Ed.), *Handbook of parapsychology* (pp.81-130). New York: Van Nostrand Reinhold.

CALKINS, J. (1980). Comments. *Zetetic Scholar*, 1(6), 77-81.

DALE, L.A. (1943). Note on an attempt to repeat the Woodworth results. *Journal of the American Society for Psychical Research*, 37, 134-137.

DALTON, K.S., MORRIS, R.L., DELANOY, D.L., RADIN, D., TAYLOR, R. and WISEMAN, R. (1994). Security measures in an automated ganzfeld system. In D.J. Bierman (Ed.), *The Parapsychological Association 37th Annual Convention: Proceedings of presented papers* (pp.114-123). Amsterdam: University of Amsterdam.

DAVIS, J.W. and AKERS, C. (1974). Randomisation and tests for randomness. *Journal of Parapsychology*, 38, 393-407.

DELANOY, D.L., WATT, C.A., MORRIS, R.L. and WISEMAN, R. (1993). A new methodology for free-response ESP testing outwith the laboratory: Findings from experienced participants. In *The Parapsychological Association 36th Annual Convention: Proceedings of presented papers* (pp.204-221).

DUNN, A.J. (1980). Neurochemistry of learning and memory: An evaluation of recent data. *Annual Review of Psychology*, 31, 343-390.

EPSTEIN, R.A. (1967). *The theory of gambling and statistical logic.* New York: Academic Press.

ESTABROOKS, G.H. (1947). *Spiritism.* New York: Dutton.

FIENBERG, S.E. (1971). Randomization and social affairs: The 1970 draft lottery. *Science*, 171, 255-261.

GARDNER, M. (1981). *Science: Good, bad, and bogus*. Buffalo, NY: Prometheus Books.

GARDNER, M. (1989). *How not to test a psychic: Ten years of remarkable experiments with renowned clairvoyant Pavel Stepanek.* Buffalo, NY: Prometheus Books.

GILMORE, J.B. (1989). Randomness and the search for psi. *Journal of Parapsychology*, 53, 309-340.

GREENWOOD, J.A. (1938). An empirical investigation of some sampling problems. *Journal of Parapsychology*, 2, 222-230.

GREVILLE, T.N.E. (1944). On multiple matching with one variable deck. *Annals of Mathematical Statistics,* 15, 432-434.

HANLON, J. (1974). Uri Geller and science. *New Scientist*, 64, 170-185.

HANSEL, C.E.M. (1959, April 30). Experiments on telepathy. *New Scientist,* 5, 983-984.

HANSEL, C.E.M. (1961). A critical analysis of the Pearce-Pratt experiment. *Journal of Parapsychology*, 25, 87-91.

HANSEL, C.E.M. (1966). *ESP: A scientific evaluation.* New York: Scribner.

HANSEL, C.E.M. (1980). *ESP and parapsychology: A critical re-evaluation.* Buffalo, NY: Prometheus Books.

HANSEL, C.E.M. (1981). A critical analysis of H. Schmidt's psychokinesis experiments. *Skeptical Inquirer,* 5, 26-33.

HANSEN, G.P. (1987). Monte Carlo methods in parapsychology. In D.H. Weiner and R.D. Nelson (Eds.), *Research in Parapsychology 1986,* (pp.93-97). Metuchen, NJ: Scarecrow Press.

HANSEN, G.P. (1990). Deception by subjects in psi research. *Journal of the American Society for Psychical Research,* 84, 25-80.

HERBERT, C.V.C. (1938). Experiment in extra-sensory perception: I. A note on types of Zener cards used at Duke University. *Journal of the Society for Psychical Research,* 32, 215-218.

HONORTON, C. (1985). Meta-analysis of psi ganzfeld research: A response to Hyman. *Journal of Parapsychology,* 49, 51-91.

HONORTON, C. and FERRARI, D.C. (1989). Meta-analysis of forced-choice precognition experiments. *Journal of Parapsychology,* 53, 281-308.

HONORTON, C., FERRARI, D.C. and BEM, D.J. (1990). Extraversion and ESP performance: A meta-analysis and a new confirmation. In *The Parapsychological Association 33rd Annual Convention: Proceedings of presented papers* (pp.113-125).

HYMAN, R. (1977a). The case against parapsychology. *The Humanist,* November/December, 47-49.

HYMAN, R. (1977b). Psychics and scientists: "Mind-Reach" and remote viewing. *The Humanist*, May/June, 16-20.

HYMAN, R. (1981). Further comments of Schmidt's PK experiments: Alternative explanations are abundant. *Skeptical Inquirer,* 5, 34-40.

HYMAN, R. (1985). The ganzfeld psi experiment: A critical appraisal. *Journal of Parapsychology,* 49, 3-49.

HYMAN, R. (1991). Comment. *Statistical Science*, 6, 389-392.

HYMAN, R. (1994). Anomaly or artifact? Comments on Bem and Honorton. *Psychological Bulletin*, 115, 19-24.

HYMAN, R. and HONORTON, C. (1986). A joint communiqué: The psi ganzfeld controversy. *Journal of Parapsychology*, 50, 350-364.

KENNEDY, J.E. (1979a). Methodological problems in free-response ESP experiments. *Journal of the American Society for Psychical Research,* 73, 1-15.

KENNEDY, J.E. (1979b). More on methodological issues in free-response psi experiments. *Journal of the American Society for Psychical Research,* 73, 395-401.

KENNEDY, J.L. (1938). The visual cues from the backs of ESP cards. *Journal of Parapsychology*, 6, 149-153.

KENNEDY, J.L. (1939a). A critical review of "Discrimination shown between experimenters by subjects" by J.D. MacFarland. *Journal of Parapsychology,* 3, 213-225.

KENNEDY, J.L. (1939b). A methodological review of extra-sensory perception. *Psychological Bulletin,* 36, 59-103.

KENNEDY, J.L. and UPHOFF, H.F. (1939). Experiments on the nature of extra-sensory perception. *Journal of Parapsychology*, 3, 226-245.

LAWRENCE, T. (1993). Gathering in the sheep and goats... A meta-analysis of forced-choice sheep-goat ESP studies, 1947-1993. In *The Parapsychological Association 36th Annual Convention: Proceedings of presented papers* (pp.75-86). The Parapsychological Association.

LEMMON, V.W. (1939). The role of selection in ESP data. *Journal of Parapsychology*, 3, 104-106.

LEUBA, C. (1938). An experiment to test the role of chance in ESP research. *Journal of Parapsychology*, 2, 217-221.

MARKS, D. and KAMMANN, R. (1978). Information transmission in remote viewing experiments [Letter]. *Nature*, 274, 680-681.

MARKS, D. and KAMMANN, R. (1980). *The psychology of the psychic*. Buffalo, NY: Prometheus Books.

MARKS, D. (1981). Sensory cues invalidate remote viewing experiments [Letter]. *Nature*, 292, 177.

MAY, E.C., HUMPHREY, B.S. and HUBBARD, G.S. (1980). *Electronic system perturbation techniques: Final report.* SRI International: Menlo Park, CA.

MILTON, J. (1993). A meta-analysis of waking state of consciousness, free-response ESP studies. In *The Parapsychological Association 36th Annual Convention: Proceedings of presented papers* (pp.87-104). The Parapsychological Association.

MILTON, J. (1994). Mass ESP: A meta-analysis of mass-media recruitment ESP studies. In D.J. Bierman (Ed.), *The Parapsychological Association 37th Annual Convention: Proceedings of presented papers* (pp.284-292). Amsterdam: The Parapsychological Association.

MILTON, J. (1995a). Issues in the adoption of methodological safeguards in parapsychology experiments. In *The Parapsychological Association 38th Annual Convention: Proceedings of presented papers.* The Parapsychological Association.

MILTON, J. (1995b). Publishing and funding parapsychology in the mainstream: A mail survey of experiences and strategies for success. *European Journal of Parapsychology*, 11, 1-18.

MILTON, J. (1996). *Establishing methodological guidelines for ESP studies: A questionnaire survey of experimenters' and critics' consensus.* Manuscript submitted for publication.

MODIANOS, D.T., SCOTT, R.C. and CORNWELL, L.W. (1984). Random number generation on microcomputers. *Interfaces,* 14, 81-87.

MORGAN, K. (1987). Anomalous Human-Computer Interaction (A.H.C.I.): Towards an understanding of what constitutes an anomaly (or how to make friends and influence computers). In *The Parapsychological Association 30th Annual Convention: Proceedings of presented papers* (pp.123-138).

MORRIS, R.L. (1978). A survey of methods and issues in ESP research. In S. Krippner (Ed.), *Advances in parapsychological research 2: Extrasensory perception* (pp.7-58). New York: Plenum.

MORRIS, R.L. (1986a). Minimizing subject fraud in parapsychology laboratories. *European Journal of Parapsychology*, 6, 137-149.

MORRIS, R.L. (1986b). What psi is not: The necessity for experiments. In H.L. Edge, R.L. Morris, J. Palmer and J.H. Rush (Eds.), *Foundations of parapsychology: Exploring the boundaries of human capability* (pp.70-110). Boston: Routledge and Kegan Paul.

MORRIS, R.L., CUNNINGHAM, S., MCALPINE, S. and TAYLOR, R. (1993). Toward replication and extension of autoganzfeld results. In *The Parapsychological Association 36th Annual Convention: Proceedings of presented papers* (pp.177-191). The Parapsychological Association.

NELSON, R.D., DUNNE, B.J. and JAHN, R.G. (1988). *Operator related anomalies in a Random Mechanical Cascade experiment* (Technical Note PEAR 88001). Princeton Engineering Anomalies Research, Princeton University, School of Engineering/Applied Science.

NICOL, J.F. (1976). The experimenter's responsibility. In M. Ebon (Ed.), *The Satan trap*. Garden City, NY: Doubleday.

PALMER, J. (1978). Extrasensory perception: Research findings. In S. Krippner (Ed.), *Advances in parapsychological research 2: Extrasensory perception* (pp.59-243). New York: Plenum Press.

PALMER, J. (1982). Methodological objections to the case for psi: Are formal control conditions necessary for the demonstration of psi? *Journal of Indian Psychology,* 4, 13-18.

PALMER, J. (1983). Sensory contamination of free-response ESP targets: The greasy fingers hypothesis. *Journal of the American Society for Psychical Research*, 77, 101-113.

PALMER, J. (1986a). Experimental methods in ESP research. In H.L. Edge, R.L. Morris, J. Palmer and J.H. Rush (Eds.), *Foundations of parapsychology: Exploring the boundaries of human capability* (pp. 111-137). Boston: Routledge and Kegan Paul.

PALMER, J. (1986b). Statistical methods in ESP research. In H.L. Edge, R.L. Morris, J. Palmer and J.H. Rush, (Eds.), *Foundations of parapsychology: Exploring the boundaries of human capability* (pp.138-160). Boston: Routledge and Kegan Paul.

PALMER, J. (1986c). Letter to the editor. *Journal of Parapsychology*, 50, 303.

PALMER, J. (1989). A reply to Gilmore. *Journal of Parapsychology,* 53, 341-344.

PALMER, J. (1996). Personal communication to authors.

PALMER, J. and KRAMER, W. (1986). Sensory identification of contaminated free-response ESP targets: Return of the greasy fingers. *Journal of the American Society for Psychical Research,* 80, 265-278.

PALMER, J. and WEINER, D.H. (1985). Technical note: A check for local singlet biases in the RAND table. *Journal of Parapsychology,* 49, 367-370.

PARAPSYCHOLOGICAL ASSOCIATION (1975). Motion concerning editorial and institutional policy. *Journal of Parapsychology*, 39, 368.

PARAPSYCHOLOGICAL ASSOCIATION (1980). *Ethical and professional standards for parapsychologists.* Alexandria, VA: Parapsychological Association.

PRATT, J.G. (1954). The variance for multiple-calling ESP data. *Journal of Parapsychology,* 18, 37-40.

Publication manual of the American Psychological Association (4th ed.) (1994). Washington, DC: American Psychological Association.

RADIN, D.I. (1985). Pseudorandom number generators in psi research. *Journal of Parapsychology*, 49, 303-328.

RADIN, D.I. and FERRARI, D.C. (1991). Effects of consciousness on the fall of dice: A meta-analysis. *Journal of Scientific Exploration,* 5, 61-83.

RAND CORPORATION (1955). *A million random digits and 100,000 normal deviates.* New York: Free Press.

RANDI, J. (1986). The role of conjurors in psi research. In P. Kurtz (Ed.), *A Skeptic's handbook of parapsychology* (pp.339-349). Buffalo, NY: Prometheus Books.

Research notes. (1938). *Journal of Parapsychology*, 2, 72-73.

RHINE, J.B. (1938). The hypothesis of deception. *Journal of Parapsychology*, 2, 151-152.

RHINE, J.B. and PRATT, J.G. (1954). A review of the Pearce-Pratt distance series of ESP tests. *Journal of Parapsychology*, 18, 165-177.

RHINE, J.B. and PRATT, J.G. (1961). A reply to the Hansel critique of the Pearce-Pratt series. *Journal of Parapsychology*, 25, 92-98.

RHINE, J.B., PRATT, J.G., SMITH, B.M., STUART, C.E. and GREENWOOD, J.A. (1966). *Extrasensory perception after sixty years.* Boston: Bruce Humphries. (Original published in 1940; New York: Henry Holt and Co.)

ROSENBLATT, J.R. and FILLIBEN, J.J. (1971). Randomization and the draft lottery. *Science*, 171, 306-308.

ROSENTHAL, R.R. (1978). How often are our numbers wrong? *American Psychologist*, 33, 1005-1008.

ROSENTHAL, R. and RUBIN, D.B. (1984). Multiple contrasts and ordered Bonferroni procedures. *Journal of Educational Psychology*, 76, 1028-1034.

SARGENT, C.L. (1980). Comments on "Effects of associations and feedback on psi in the ganzfeld" [Letter]. *Journal of the American Society for Psychical Research,* 74, 265-267.

SCHMEIDLER, G.R. (1977). Methods for controlled research on ESP and PK. In B.B. Wolman (Ed.), *Handbook of parapsychology* (pp.131-159). New York: Van Nostrand Reinhold.

SCHMEIDLER, G.R. (1994). Personal communication to first author.

SCHMEIDLER, G.R. and LINDEMANN, C. (1966). ESP calls following an "ESP" test with sensory cues. *Journal of the American Society for Psychical Research,* 60, 357-362.

SCHMIDT, H. (1970). Quantum-mechanical random-number generator. *Journal of Applied Physics,* 41(2), 462-468.

SCHOUTEN, S.A. (1975). Effect of reducing response preferences on ESP scores. *European Journal of Parapsychology*, 1, 60-66.

SCOTT, C. and GOLDNEY, K.M. (1960). The Jones boys and the ultra-sonic whistle. *Journal of the Society for Psychical Research,* 40, 249-260.

SOAL, S.G. and BOWDEN, H.T. (1960). *The mind readers*. Garden City, NY: Doubleday.

SOMMER, R. and SOMMER, B. (1983). Mystery in Milwaukee. *American Psychologist,* 38, 982-985.

SPENCER-BROWN, G. (1957). *Probability and scientific inference.* London and New York: Longmans Green.

STANFORD, R.G. (1990, January). Secretary's report, 1989. *PA News and Annual Report*. Durham, NC: The Parapsychological Association, Inc.

STANFORD, R.G. and STEIN, A.G. (1994). A meta-analysis of ESP studies contrasting hypnosis and a comparison condition. *Journal of Parapsychology,* 58, 235-269.

STEVENSON, I. (1967). An antagonist's view of parapsychology. A review of Professor Hansel's *ESP: A Scientific Evaluation. Journal of the American Society for Psychical Research*, 61, 254-267.

STOKES, D. (1978). Review of *Research in Parapsychology 1976*, edited by J.D. Morris, W.G. Roll and R.L. Morris. *Journal of Parapsychology,* 42, 70-76.

TARG, R. and PUTHOFF, H. (1974). Information transmission under conditions of sensory shielding. *Nature*, 252, 602-607.

TART, C.T. and DRONEK, E. (1982). Mathematical inference strategies versus psi: Initial explorations with the Probabilistic Predictor Program. *European Journal of Parapsychology*, 4, 325-355.

The ESP symposium at the A.P.A.(1938).*Journal of Parapsychology,* 2, 247-272.

TYRRELL, G.N.M. (1938). The Tyrrell apparatus for testing extra-sensory perception. *Journal of Parapsychology*, 2, 107-118.

UTTS, J. (1991). Replication and meta-analysis in parapsychology. *Statistical Science*, 6, 363-403.

WAGENAAR, W.A. (1972). Generation of random sequences by human subjects: A critical survey of the literature. *Psychological Bulletin,* 77, 65-72.

WEINER, D.H. (1995). Personal communication to first author.

WISEMAN, R., BELOFF, J. and MORRIS, R.L. (1992). Testing the ESP claims of SORRAT. *Journal of the Society for Psychical Research*, 58, 363-377.

WISEMAN, R. and MORRIS, R.L. (1995). *Guidelines for testing psychic claimants.* Hatfield, UK: University of Hertfordshire Press.

WISEMAN, R., SMITH, M.D. and KORNBROT, D. (1996). Exploring possible sender-to-experimenter acoustic leakage in the PRL autoganzfeld experiments. *Journal of Parapsychology*, 60, 97-128.

Methodological checklist

Some of the checklist items deal with safeguards necessary for experimental procedures that most experimenters would want to avoid but that some use because of participants' assumed or stated psychological requirements. Generally speaking, the more that procedures attempt to mimic ordinary sensory perception by having targets on display somewhere, or having a sender aware of the target identity, or having the target near the receiver, the more safeguards are required and the harder it is to be sure that those safeguards are sufficient. For example, if a target is on open display in a room (other than the receiver's, of course), complete protection of that target would involve having all access points to the room, including windows and trapdoors, secured or guarded against an accomplice gaining entry or peeking.

It is much easier for an experimenter to sit and guard a target that is in a sealed, opaque package and such a procedure is both more convincingly effective and quicker and easier to describe in the experimental report. Unless researchers have a compelling reason for using the more difficult procedures, we recommend that they save time, effort, expense and journal space by using procedures that are easy to safeguard.

The reader should refer to the main body of the text for a reminder of the rationale for each safeguard and the amount of published support there is for it. To provide an indicator of the amount of unpublished support among researchers who have recently published ESP studies or critiques of ESP experimental methodology, the first author conducted a questionnaire survey among twenty-eight such researchers (Milton, 1996). If over 50 per cent of respondents considered a safeguard procedure necessary (that is, that the procedure, if followed, would have led them to take any positive results in an experiment seriously enough to recommend the paper for publication, assuming that the other procedures in the experiment were carried out to their satisfaction), then the safeguard is marked 'A'. Those safeguards that the greater number considered at least desirable (that the respondent would have preferred to be carried out, and reported if journal space permitted, but that would not be crucial in their assessment of a paper) are maked 'B'. Safeguards that respondents thought unnecessary are marked 'C'. Safeguards not marked were not included in the questionnaire.

Pre-specification of experimental details and statistical tests

- Pre-specify in writing before the experiment how many trials will be conducted (or if testing groups whose size is not known in advance, as in classroom testing, pre-specify the number of groups).[A]

- Pre-specify in writing whether any surplus back-up trials will be included in data analysis.

- Pre-specify any study's status (as exploratory, confirmatory, etc.).

- Decide in advance which, if any, trials are to be considered 'practice' trials and which experimental trials, and pre-specify this in writing on the trial record sheet.[A]

- Before data collection, pre-specify in writing the exact form of planned statistical analyses, including the level of alpha and whether tests are one- or two-tailed, and state in the report which analyses were pre-planned and which post-hoc.[A]

- Pre-specify in writing the type of randomness tests to be used and the output to be tested.[B]

- When multiple analysis will be an issue in interpreting results, pre-specify in writing which, if any, analyses are to be considered the main analyses and the method of correction for multiple analysis, if one is to be applied.[A]

- If analyses involve examining the relationship between ESP performance and a participant's classification in terms of some other variable, specify the classification criteria in writing before the experiment.[A]

- Register the written specifications of the study's crucial procedures with someone who is otherwise uninvolved in the experiment before data collection begins.[B]

Methods of Randomisation

- Do not rely on human choice to produce target sequences. Note: this includes not allowing choice to determine the exact content of free-response targets that have already been randomly chosen, as might happen if a random number generator was used to select the page of a dictionary and the target was to be a picture depicting the meaning of the first drawable word. The judgment of which words were drawable would introduce an element of choice, as would the decision of how to depict the word's meaning.

Dice-throwing, card-shuffling and drawing lots

- Even assuming that they pass randomness tests, do not use manual forms of randomisation such as card-shuffling, dice-throwing and the drawing of lots as sources of randomisation.[A]

Mechanical and electronic RNGs

- Describe the physics of the RNG and its operational paramenters in sufficient detail for the potential impact of enviromental factors to be assessed.[B]

- Give the model name of an electronic RNG and the full reference to its description, including its circuit diagram if one has been published.[B] For a mechanical RNG, provide or refer to details of its construction, including diagrams and plans.

- Give the model name of any computer interfaced with the RNG.

- Shield an electronic RNG against transient magnetic field changes, power spikes, etc.[C]

Pseudo-RNGs

- Do not use a microcomputer random function as an RNG unless its algorithm is documented and tests have shown that it is adequately random.

- Report full details of the procedure for choosing the seed number.[A]

- Report the full reference of the pseudo-RNG programme.[A]

- Report the pseudo-RNG programme and details of the statistical tests conducted upon it (or give references to this information).

- If the pseudo-RNG programme is not being run in the experiment under the same hardware and software conditions as obtained during the randomness tests, compare the first 50 numbers generated by it for a particular seed number under both randomness testing and experimental conditions to check that the programme's output is identical under both conditions.

- Do not use informal methods of randomisation to select the seed number if a different seed number is being produced to choose each trial's target, rather than one seed number for the whole study.

Random number tables

- Use a random number table that thorough testing shows is adequately random, such as the RAND Corporation (1955) tables.

- Report the full reference of the table.[A]

- Report full details of the procedure for choosing the entry point into the table.[A]

- Use the digits in the table in the order in which they have been tested for randomness, i.e. if they have been tested row by row, use them in that order and not column by column.[A]

- Do not use informal methods of randomisation to select the entry point into the table if a different entry point is being produced to choose each trial's target, rather than one entry point for the whole study.

Randomiser details

- Report details of the randomiser's training and qualifications relevant to his or her ability to carry out the procedure correctly.[C]

Randomness Testing

When, how and where tests should be conducted

- Test an RNG extensively before using it in experiments and at regular intervals thereafter.

- Test the RNG for randomness under the same conditions that might affect it as those present during the experiment. For mechanical or electronic RNGs this means testing under the same range of temperature, humidity and other environmental factors[C] and, for electronic RNGs, at the same rate of operation[A] and in situ with the same peripherals connected[A]. For a pseudo-RNG, this involves using the same hardware and software conditions.[A]

- During any multiple-block randomisation tests (i.e. tests in which multiple blocks of output roughly the same length as the experimental series are tested for randomness) have an electronic RNG switched on and running for each block only for the same period of time as it is during the experimental trials to detect transient effects on the device when it is switched on and off and warming up.[A]

- During any multiple-block randomisation tests with an electronic RNG, generate the blocks as near to the time of the experimental trials as possible.[B]

- Repeat the randomness tests if the RNG has been replaced or modified before the experiment.[A]

Choice of output: Global or local?

- Conduct randomness tests both on a series of the RNG's output much longer than the experimental target sequence and on the experimental target sequence itself (or, if the target sequence is too short for tests to be meaningful, on multiple blocks of output the same length as the target sequence instead).[A]

- In studies with trial-by-trial feedback, randomness tests restricted to the experiment's target sequence only are insufficient to demonstrate that there was no pattern that receivers could have detected and exploited and so tests of the RNG's parent distribution are necessary.

Coding the output

- If you use a code to transform the raw output of an RNG into a sequence of targets with fewer alternatives than the RNG produces (e.g. if the RNG produces the digits 0-9 and you use a code such as '0' or '5' to mean that the target is 'circle', '1' or '6' to mean that the target is 'cross' and so on, so that the ten digits become only five target alternatives) then subject the coded output rather than the raw output to randomness tests.[C]

- Report the exact method of translating the RNG's output into the target sequence.

Choice of randomness tests

- Perform frequency tests of the occurence of each digit.[A]

- Perform frequency tests of the occurence of each possible pairing of digits of at least lag 1 and up to lag 10.

- Even if randomness tests prove satisfactory, carry out an 'empirical cross-check' of receivers' responses with the targets of trials for which those responses had not been intended.[C]

Reporting of randomness tests

- Report randomness tests alongside the experimental results.

Type of Participant

Extent of experimental safeguards against cheating

- Take precautions against opportunistic cheating (e.g. trying to peek inside target containers, altering accessible experimental records) even for unselected participants who are contributing one trial each to a study with many trials.[A]

- Take additional precautions against forms of cheating that would involve planning, special skills or the use of an accomplice, for any participant known or suspected to use or be knowledgeable about trickery, or who has made public claims of 'psychic' abilities or who will be the sole participant in a study.

- In studies with special participants, use videotaping and other media to record the study's procedures.

Participant information: Special participants

- Report details of the participant's background in using or studying trickery or of being suspected of doing so.[A]

- Describe any suspicious behaviour during the experiment, even if there was no firm proof of cheating.[A]

- Make public any clear evidence of cheating in the study if the participant has made public claims of psychic abilities.

- Report the participant's name.[C]

- Report details of any public claims of 'psychic' abilities made by the participant.[A]

- Cite any published accounts of the participant's attempted 'psychic' feats or previous experimental participation, whether successful or not.[A]

- Do not rely upon the participant for details of his or her background and history or even for his or her true name.

- Report whether the magicians in the participant's local community are aware of him or her having studied magic.[B]

- State whether the major magical organisations report that the participant is or was one of their members.[B]

- If computer security is an issue, report participants' knowledge of computers and programming.[B]

- Report details of any modifications to the participipant's original claim during pilot testing and any departures from planned procedure.

- Give details of any agreement between experimenter and participant concerning how the results of the study will be used (e.g. whether the participant will be free to use a sucessful outcome for self-advertisement).

- If target security depends upon the experimenter closely monitoring the receiver's actions, report details of the experimenter's background in conjuring and ability to make the crucial observations.[A]

Participant details: All studies

- Report results individually for each participant.

- Report what proportion of receiver-sender pairs were friends.[A]

Sensory Shielding I: Pre-Trial Safeguards

Safeguards before target selection

- If targets are generated by means of a mechanical or electronic (including computer) random number generator, prevent participants from gaining access to the generator and tampering with it.[A]

- Do not publish accounts of a laboratory's randomisation procedure that would allow participants to reconstruct their target sequence or target identity.[A]

Safeguards during target selection

- Have the randomising experimenter prepare the targets alone in an adequately visually shielded room.[A]

Safeguards after target selection

Shielding target-identifying materials from receivers

- Immediately the targets have been selected, shield the receiver from any information concerning the target's identity (e.g. target lists, remaining control items in a current free-response trial's target set, sheets of paper from underneath the target record that might bear impressions of the writing, etc.).[A]

- Report details of how targets are kept secure between being taken out of storage and being used in the trial.[A]

- For special claimants, consider storing target records by using special containers with tamper-evident devices and, for computer-held information, using VDU screen shielding, applying cryptographic methods and/or preventing cable monitoring.

- If security will depend upon the integrity of a target container's seal, check the container's sealing mechanism before use to ensure that it has not been tampered with in such a way that it could be breached undetectably.

Shielding non-blind laboratory personnel from receivers

- Allow the percipient no contact before or during the trial with an experimenter who knows the target identity.

- Do not allow experimenters who are with receivers before or during the trial to have any sensory contact with the target (e.g. to shuffle cards without looking at them).

- Do not allow receivers to have contact with anyone who has seen targets being placed into their containers.[A]

- When an intermediary who knows the target identity is required to give to the experimenter an opaque package containing the target, while the experimenter is blind to its contents, prevent the intermediary from speaking to or being seen by the experimenter,[A] from giving accidental auditory cues, or from being free to place the package freely in such a way that position cues might be available.

Sensory Shielding II: Safeguards During the Trial

In this section it is assumed that targets consist of written or pictorial material (pictures, cards, sheets of paper bearing target lists, etc.). Additional precautions are likely to be necessary under most circumstances if using other types of target such as objects, people, music and so on.

Shielding targets from receivers

- Have the receiver supervised by an experimenter during the trial.

- Report who was present during experimental trials and how supervision of any non-laboratory personnel was maintained.[A]

Clairvoyance studies with target in same room as receiver

- Place targets inside opaque containers rather than using partial screening or blindfolds.

- Report details of the materials and construction of the target containers and, if appropriate, how they were tested for opacity.[A]

- In experiments in which the receiver gets target feedback, do not permit receivers or any possible accomplices to either see or handle any target container that will be re-used in later trials to contain the same target.[A]

Clairvoyance studies with target within receiver's reach

- Make the target container proof against being rendered

transparent by the application of water, alcohol or oil or by having a bright point light source held directly behind it.[A]

- If free-response targets in a target set differ in weight, size or other characteristics that might be used by the judge to distinguish them, ensure that such differences are not apparent once the target is in the container.[A]

- Seal the target container in such a way that tampering would be detected.[A]

- The experimenter, not the receiver, must open the target container at the end of the trial, following a pre-specified checking procedure to examine the container for signs of tampering.[A]

- Place secret marks or codes on the target container so that the experimenter can detect a receiver's attempts to replace a breached container with a similar one.[A]

Shielding senders from receivers

- Do not allow either the sender or the sender's experimenter to signal their readiness for a trial once they know the target (use automatic signalling or receiver-to-sender signalling instead).[A]

- Instruct the sender to be as quiet and still as possible.[B]

- Supervise the sender in such a way that obvious attempts to signal to the receiver, or to interfere with the shielding between them, would be detected.[A]

- Have the sender and receiver in different rooms with at least one other room between them.[A]

- Ensure that visual screening prevents the receiver from seeing the sender's movements, shadows under the sender's door or changes in illumination in the sender's room, including by means of reflecting surfaces.[A]

- Report sufficient detail for readers to assess whether sound or vibration could carry between the sender's room and the receiver's (relative position of the rooms, number and construction of intervening partitions, type of floor, whether the rooms are connected by heating pipes, ventilation ducts, etc.).[A]

- Carry out informal tests to see if sound or vibration from the sender's room, similar in pitch but greater in volume than any that the sender would make under supervision, could be heard in the receiver's room.[A]

- Even if informal tests reveal no problem, carry out objective, instrumented tests.[B]

- Whatever type of shielding is being used to screen the receiver, assess its effectiveness at the time of testing in case it has been modified over time.

- In studies in which the experimenter is present when the receiver makes his or her response, shield the experimenter adequately from the target (and sender if there is one).

Shielding accomplices from receivers

- When the target is in another room from the percipient, secure or guard all access points to the target room (door, windows, trapdoors) in such a way that entry would be detected.[A]

- If the target is on display, screen or guard the room against peeking.[A]

- If the target is on display, supervise the room, or choose a room constructed or positioned so that no modifications could be made to it, without attracting attention, that would allow peeking (e.g. rubbing blackout off windows, poking holes in board walls or trapdoors, etc.)[A]

- If a sender is present who might collude with a receiver to cheat, then visual and auditory shielding, and supervision, should be sufficient to prevent an accomplice from detecting signals from the sender.[A]

- Take precautions against cheating by radio communication when the target is not well-secured against a possible accomplice (e.g. by means of a Faraday cage, the use of only laboratory personnel as senders or the use of electronic counter-surveillance) for any participant known or suspected to use or be knowledgeable about trickery, or who has made public claims of 'psychic' abilities, or who is the sole participant in the study.[A]

Sensory Shielding III: Post-Trial Safeguards

Post-trial target shielding

- Keep shielding and supervision of the target (and sender, if there is one) in place until the receiver's response has been secured.[A]

- Secure the record of the receiver's responses before feedback is given and do not allow the receiver to alter, add to or have access to the response record after it has been secured.[A]

- Take measures to prevent the sender from substituting another item for the real target and having the substitute used as the basis for determining the trial's outcome (e.g. cross-check the target with the laboratory record of what it should be).[A]

Post-trial target record shielding

- Store records of experimental data, including those stored on computer, with appropriate security as they are accumulated. If further caution is indicated, continuously update duplicate data summary records and have them held by more than one laboratory member, to be cross-checked at the end of the experiment.[A]

- Keep any written experimental records in indelible ink.

Free-Response Judging

Blind transcription, transcription checking, response handling and judging

- If it is necessary to transcribe the receiver's mentation for later use by a judge (including the receiver, if he or she is to be the judge), have the transcription done by someone who is blind to the target's identity.[A]

- If the transcript is to be checked for accuracy (e.g. against the receiver's memory of what was said, against an audiotape of the receiver's verbalised mentation report, or against the original of a mentation report that has been translated into a foreign language), have the checking also done by someone who is blind to the target's identity.[A]

- The judge should not have contact with anyone who knows the target identities (or target orders, for a closed-deck study).[A]

- Instructions to the judges must be given or written by someone who is blind to the target identities.[A]

- Prevent anyone, including experimenters, who know the target's identity, from handling response sheets or transcripts that have yet to be judged.

Handling cues

- Give the judge duplicate judging sets rather than the original target sets to avoid cues from handling.[A] Note that this recommendation applies not only to telepathy studies but to all studies in which anyone, including any laboratory personnel, handles the target (to place it in an opaque package, for example). In studies in which duplicate sets are not possible, such as studies employing unique objects as targets, target handling by senders should be avoided. However, in telepathy studies where handling cannot be ruled out (e.g. if targets are geographical sites, where the sender could unobtrusively leave markers), use independent rather than receiver judging.

Cues from contemporaneous target description

- If descriptions of the target set are to be used in the judging process (e.g. if the judge is presented with descriptions or photographs of a number of geographical locations, one of which is the target), have these descriptions prepared in advance of the experiment rather than being made contemporary with, or in the same order, as the trials.[A]

Ordering of items within the judging set

- The position of the target in the set must be random when it is presented to the judge: in a closed-deck experiment, present each trial's target in random order with respect to the order of presentation of each trial's mentation transcript.[A]

- Randomise the position of the target in the judging set using a randomisation source that would be considered sufficiently random to generate the target sequence itself.[A]

- In a closed-deck experiment, the targets (or target descriptions) must not bear any information that would enable them to be placed in order of use, or matched against trial-identifying information on the mentation transcripts such as the date of the trial, the time of day, the trial number, the participant's code number, the experimenter's code number, etc. Describe how targets were coded for presentation to the judges and how the order of presentation was determined.[A]

Cues from length of target presentation

- If targets within a judging set differ in presentation length (e.g. if targets consist of movie clips or audio tracks), the length of presentation must not be allowed to determine the length of the receiver's response period and the receiver must be blind to presentation length.[A]

Cues due to feedback

- Do not use closed-deck procedures if trial-by-trial feedback is given and if receivers in the study do more than one trial.[A]

- In closed-deck studies, receivers' experimenters should also receive no feedback of target identities until after response records for the whole study have been secured.

- In open-deck studies with trial-by-trial feedback, prevent judges from basing their choice of target for a trial on a receiver's mentioning that trial's target in the transcripts of later trials. Have judges judge transcripts one at a time in order and prevent them from altering their judgments after seeing later transcripts.

- If relying upon judges in an open-deck study with trial-by-trial feedback and unedited transcipts to follow instructions not to go back and change an earlier judgment in the light of information about earlier targets in transcripts of later trials, only use named judges who are laboratory personnel, or other people involved in academic research who can be relied upon to understand the reasons for the instructions and respect those reasons. It is not sufficient to use judges recruited in the same way as experimental participants (e.g. students, volunteers from the community, etc).[A]

Recording, Checking, Scoring and Calculation Procedures

Target transcription errors

- If the target identity is not recorded by automation but must be recorded by an experimenter (e.g. if targets are transcribed from a random number generator that is not hooked up to a computer), have the target transcription checked for accuracy by either the original transcriber or, for a more stringent safeguard,[A] by another person.

Target and response recording

- Use automated or computerised data recording and handling if possible.

- If automation is used, provide details of checks that it is functioning properly.

- Do not allow experimental participants to record or check data (except for receivers recording their own responses while blind to the target and only if the experimenter secures the response record before feedback).

- Keep the person who records the target identity (including the randomiser in precognition studies) blind to the receiver's reponse, and the person who records the receiver's response blind to the target.[A]

Scoring and counting of hits

- If the designation of each trial's outcome (as a hit or miss, or rank, etc.) is not automated, it is necessary to have the designation checked by either the original designator or, more stringently,[A] by another person (but not the receiver or sender).

- If a different person from the original outcome designator is to perform the check, keep him or her blind to the original designator's scoring.

- If the original outcome designator performs the check, the original scoring should be concealed and the task undertaken only after some time has lapsed or a similar task has intervened to lessen the effects of memory.

Data entry for computation

- When data is transferred from individual record sheets to raw data summary tables or computer tables that will be used to make statistical calculations, have the tables double-checked against the originals, preferably by someone other than the person who transferred the data.

Checker details

- Provide the names and training and qualification details of the personnel who carry out the data recording and handling procedures.[C]

Checking of statistical calculations

- Have the experimenter's statistical calculations checked either by the experimenter[A] or, for a more stringent check, by another person.

Reporting and Retaining Data

Selective reporting of trials

- If, during a trial, it transpires that the trial is not to be considered part of the experiment (if, for example, the experiment is one in which receivers are allowed to 'pass' on some trials, or if a trial is aborted halfway through, for some reason), this decision should be recorded in writing by the experimenter before either receiver or experimenter receive feedback of the target's identity.[A]

- If, after a trial has ended and feedback has been received, it is discovered that some circumstance requires the trial not to be included in the experiment (for example, if an electronic RNG is found to have developed a fault), give the reason for the exclusion in the report and report the data from the excluded trials.[A]

- If fewer trials have been carried out in a study than planned, justify the shortfall of trials and report how many are missing. Consider correcting for the missing trials in the overall outcome measure by assuming that they yielded chance scoring.

- If a receiver drops out of a repeated-measures study, the reason should be reported and his or her data presented.[A]

Selective reporting of studies

- Do not base a decision to publish a study on whether the results are statistically significant.

Retaining data

- Retain all raw data and experimental records for at least five years after publication of the report in a journal affiliated to the American Psychological Association, or after presentation of the report at the Parapsychological Association annual convention.

Other Considerations

Experimenter fraud

- Consider taking measures against experimenter fraud.

Consultation with magicians

- When testing a participant who has made strong claims of 'psychic' abilities and who is the sole participant in an ESP study (or one of very few), seek the advice of a suitably competent magician in order to identify weaknesses in the procedure that a magically skilled or determined participant might exploit.[B]

'Non-ESP' control condition

- A 'non-ESP' control condition to provide an empirical chance baseline for ESP studies is neither generally called for nor apparently conceptually possible but authors submitting papers outside the specialist parapsychology journals are recommended to justify the lack of such a control condition to pre-empt criticism from those unfamiliar with the issues.

Statistics

- Obtain any necessary statistical advice for non-standard experiments before finalising the study's design and ask that advice from statisticians who have a special interest in parapsychology.

- If using the normal approximation to the binomial distribution, do not omit the continuity correction. Most statistical texts recommend using the normal approximation only if $Np > 10$ and p is not extremely small (say, .05 or less), where N is the number of trials and p the probability of a hit.

- In a study where several receivers are guessing a single target sequence, as opposed to each receiver having his or her own target sequence, correction must be made for the 'stacking effect'. (See Greville (1944) for a technical discussion and Pratt (1954) for a less demanding version and worked examples.)

- If using Fisher's exact probability test, remember to add in the probabilities of getting results even more extreme than the actual outcome.

- In a free-response experiment with a closed deck and trial-by-trial feedback (not a recommended combination, see the earlier section on free-response judging), do not use statistical procedures that assume that each trial's data is independent.